"I am excited about 'Change Your Story' by Pastor Art Sepulveda. What a great read! So often when people talk about change, they tend to put you down. But Pastor Art brings you up and encourages you to never settle for less than God's best. Why? Because God has good plans for you and He created you to live an extraordinary life—not one of mediocrity or one without hope. There is great freedom and wisdom in this book, straight from the Word of God, that will empower you to do just that: change your story! This is a book you will read again and again, and one you will want to share with others. You'll be blessed by it!"

JESSE DUPLANTIS *Author, Speaker, TV Host; President and*
Founder of Jesse Duplantis Ministries

"Art Sepulveda's new book, 'Change Your Story,' is a true encouragement for anyone who, like me many years ago, finds him- or herself in what looks like an impossible situation. As Pastor Art points out so clearly, there is no such thing in the eyes of Jesus as an insignificant person. This is an easy to read, easy to comprehend, step by step guide to a fabulous new life. I wholeheartedly recommend it."

KENNETH COPELAND *Author, Speaker, TV Host; President and*
Founder of Kenneth Copeland Ministries

"Art Sepulveda's 'Change Your Story' is a powerful new book that sets the stage for an extraordinary comeback in the reader's life. Art does a masterful job showing, through Scripture and testimony, that you are never stuck where you are and that God wants to take you to an incredible new place in your life. No matter where you might be in life, 'Change Your Story' will inspire and embolden you to take the next big step into new and exciting things."

MATTHEW BARNETT *Co-founder of The Dream Center*

"Everyone's life is a story in the making, and that story can have either a happy or sad ending. When we try to handle our lives all by ourselves, without divine intervention, we can get overwhelmed. No matter how hard we try or how good our intentions are, discouragement can make us feel like life has handed us a raw deal. It's a helpless, frustrating feeling when we think we're the tail end instead of the head.

"That's why I'm so excited about Pastor Art Sepulveda's new book, 'Change Your Story.' In it, this powerful man of God reveals the truth about how to change your life's story from a position of failure and struggling to one of victory and power. Jesus came that we might not only have life, but have it more abundantly. The people who chose to follow Him were the ones whose life stories were radically rewritten, and He's still rewriting lives today!

"God can't be contained, and therefore, we don't have to settle for being boxed in by pain, fear, or negativity. He frees us like no one else can, and reveals to us the beautiful love story He has envisioned for our life. 'Change Your Story' is a must-read!"

CREFLO DOLLAR *Senior Pastor, World Changers Church International*

"Pastor Art brings a fresh and exciting look at how we see our lives. You will be inspired to believe that God will write a successful end to your story. Worry and fear will not decide your future. Faith and vision will. The Bible is full of stories of those who started in distress but ended in success. It may seem like you are losing your battles, but take heart. As you read, you will be lifted to see what your future can be. Pastor Art has a unique ability to bring you to a new place in your life!"

CASEY TREAT *Senior Pastor, Christian Faith Center*

"Pastor Art is a change agent. When people encounter him and the message he brings, they see a change for good take place. This book will empower you to see change in your own life . . . to create history."

RUSSELL EVANS *Senior Pastor, Planetshakers Church*

"Pastor Art Sepulveda is a blessing to everyone he encounters. His positive persona and desire to see each person encouraged that God is not finished writing and re-writing the story of their lives will bring you great hope and freedom, as you lean into his wisdom and authentic teaching."

BRIAN HOUSTON *Global Senior Pastor and Founder of Hillsong Church*
International best-selling author of LIVE, LOVE, LEAD

"Everyone has a unique story. Some of us are at the start, and some in the middle, but there is never an end to your story as it is eternal in its impact. No matter where you are, you can change your story. Humans are the only beings who can do that.

"Art Sepulveda has written a classic on this vital subject. Read it. Absorb it. Apply the words that flow with wisdom, and your story will be a legacy to others."

PAT MESITI *Motivational Speaker, Mesiti.com*

"Pastor Art is a top-level inspirational speaker and a passionate communicator of the very Good News of the gospel. In this timely book he powerfully and personally applies the great Bible truths of grace, hope, and love and the limitless possibilities of new beginnings for anyone and everyone through Jesus Christ."

WES RICHARDS *Senior Pastor, King's Church International, Windsor, England*
Author of "Hope and a Future"

"I have known my very close friend Art Sepulveda for more than 35 years, and I have had the privilege of watching him and his lovely wife, Kuna, take the principles found in God's Word and totally transform their lives. In his new book, 'Change Your Story,' Art has tapped into one of God's great truths—a truth upon which every believer can build a new life that leads to fulfillment, purpose, and joy. He shares the power found in overcoming how your current thinking limits you—how the things of the past (negative circumstances, negative words, personal failures) keep you bound and hinder you from obtaining the "good life" God has prepared for you according to Ephesians 2:10.

"Would you like to see your story change? This is the book for you. God has ordained your life to be outstanding—to be a testimony to His goodness. Meditate on the truths Pastor Art shares and get ready to enjoy life better than you've ever imagined!"

JERRY SAVELLE *President and Founder of Jerry Savelle Ministries International*

ART SEPÚLVEDA

CHANGE YOUR STORY

GOD REWROTE THE TEXT OF MY LIFE
WHEN I OPENED THE BOOK OF MY HEART

CHANGE YOUR STORY

Published by WORD OF LIFE HAWAII
www.wordoflifehawaii.com

Manuscript prepared by Todd Hafer

Cover and Interior Design by Peter Gloege | LOOK Design Studio

20 19 18 17 16 [WRZ] 10 9 8 7 6 5 4 3 2 1

I dedicate this book to
the "Story Changers" of my life.

First, my family. Beginning with the love of my life,
my wife, Rochelle Kukunaokala.
My children: Ashley, Nicole (and her husband,
Branson), Alexis, and Natalie. And of course, my
grandchildren: Isabella, Isaac, and Bailee Rose.

No story is changeable without the ultimate
Story Changer of all humanity,
my Lord and Savior Jesus Christ,
for whom I am eternally and humbly grateful.

Then there's my spiritual father,
Pastor Cesar Castellanos.
The story of my life changed as a man, husband, father,
pastor and leader due to his unrelenting personal
dedication to my life. My honor and respect for my
pastor's wisdom will forever be irrevocable.

ACKNOWLEDGMENT:

Behind every great dream there is a team
of people working to bring it to pass.
I would like to give special thanks to my
"story changers" team who helped
make this book possible:
Pastor Candis Chang, Jonell Cockett,
Pastor Davin Yokomori and Sharla Nunes.

CONTENTS

FOREWORD

By Pastor Cesar Castellanos

You Can Change Your Life

The primary purpose of Jesus' redeeming work on the Cross of Calvary was to forgive our sins and to give us eternal life. "In him we have redemption through his blood, the forgiveness of sins, in accordance with the riches of God's grace" (Ephesians 1:7). He gave His life so we could have a new life, regardless of what we have been through in the past. Moses, Peter, and Paul were men who came from a history of pain, strife, let-down, persecution, and murder. Moses had to flee his country because he murdered a man. His character was weak, and he decided to take vengeance into his own hands. His future was to be far away from his own people. It was supposed to be a hopeless future.

After Peter experienced the unconditional love of Jesus, he still denied Him publicly. All he had left after that was to hide away from God's calling.

Paul, believing it was the right thing to do, dedicated his life to persecuting Christians. He constantly threatened the early Christians and approved the public stoning of Stephen. But Moses, Peter, and Paul alike discovered that, in God, their stories could change. Moses became the deliverer who freed more than three million people and took them to the Promised Land. God used him to write the first five books of the Bible. Through Moses, many wonders came to pass, like the splitting of the Red Sea, water flowing from a rock, and manna coming down from heaven every day. All because he believed that God could change his story. Through Peter's message, more than three thousand people accepted Jesus on the day of Pentecost. Later, five thousand people accepted Jesus. Even though Peter was taken to prison, the angels would show up and open up the gates in a supernatural way to free him. Nowadays when we think about Peter, we think of the man who started the Gentile church, all because he believed that God could change his story. Paul was the one who provided the excellent description of true love, found in 1 Corinthians 13, because he was able to truly experience being set free from condemnation. By believing that God could change his story and forgive the mistakes of his past, he became the author of most of the books in the New Testament.

The Lord has placed this book in your hands because He wants you to know that you can change your story. Regardless of the pain you have experienced, when His love is poured out upon your life, your biggest scars become your biggest trophies. Pastor Art is a living example of what God can do when we believe Him. He went from being a young man who longed to serve Jesus to now being a pastor of nations. His anointed words are filled with God's power, and will bring healing to your heart. Now, holding this book in your hands, you will be able to feel the Holy Spirit come upon you and bring the hope of blessing. He will bring new dreams and a desire to live your future under His blessing. Today, if you place your life in the hands of the Creator, and allow the Father to form your life, He will use your life so that thousands more can also change their stories.

Cesar Castellanos

Founder and Senior Pastor of International
Charismatic Mission, G12 Vision

INTRODUCTION

Frustrated in his dreams to become an Air Force pilot, a near-sighted California truck driver decided to explore the friendly skies his own way—with a lawn chair and 42 weather balloons filled with helium. In 1982, Larry Walters and his girlfriend attached the balloons to an aluminum lawn chair, along with some water jugs for ballast. For his flight, Walters packed a pellet pistol to shoot the balloons and control his descent—as well as a CB radio and some sandwiches and beer.

Walters planned to drift along at about 30 feet, but when he cut his craft loose from its moorings, he shot skyward at the rate of a thousand feet a minute. He didn't level off until he'd hit 16,000 feet.

Soon, he found himself drifting into the flight paths of incoming planes at Los Angeles International Airport. He used his radio to transmit a mayday call, which was received by operators on the ground. He calmly told the operators that he was in trouble one way or the other. He would either plunge to his death or get sucked into the engine of a large airliner.

Meanwhile, an airline captain radioed his tower that he had just passed a man in a lawn chair at 16,000 feet—and that the man appeared to be holding a pistol.

Eventually, Walters shot a few balloons. He began a slow descent, but he dropped the pistol before he could shoot any more. (He also lost his glasses at some point during his flight.)

During the descent, some of the tethers hanging from the balloons became tangled in power lines, knocking out the electricity in a Long Beach neighborhood. The chair was dangling just 5 feet off the ground when Walters was rescued by members of the Los Angeles Police Department, about 90 minutes after liftoff.

When asked by a reporter why he had attempted something so foolhardy, Walters replied, "A man just can't sit around."

Walters was arrested and eventually charged with unlawfully operating an aircraft in LAX airspace and "operating a civil aircraft for which there is not currently in effect an Airworthiness Certificate."

"Lawnchair Larry's" five minutes of fame included a few TV appearances and recognition from The Darwin Awards and The Bonehead Club of Dallas.

Lawnchair Larry is an extreme example of how much people want to change their lives, improve their life stories. How much they want to break free from their limitations.

The story of Lawnchair Larry is fun to read, but I prefer stories of redemption. Stories of real people—of real lives and real change. These stories portray how people are experiencing what they once thought utterly unimaginable, unthinkable, and impossible.

The secret? Well, it's not some "Wonder Drug." I'm talking about the breakthrough opportunity that God gives to every person—the opportunity to *"Change Their Story."*

Every "change of story" is born out of an inward, divine drive that begins deep in the heart. I call it "desire." This instinctive quest that compels us is undeniably eternal. Whether people credit God or not, the divine inward drive and desire is what moves us to press on, pursue, and push beyond the negative obstacles that many people too easily accept. Nobody really wants a mediocre life. We all want more than the status quo, the average, and the "good enough" patterns of living that we are often stuck with.

Yet, regardless of life's circumstances and challenges, the good news is that you can *change your story.* Nothing is impossible with God. No matter how life looks or feels.

A change of story is not the work of human hands, but rather God's hands. This is not about hype. It's not about techniques that tickle the soul but leave the deepest part of the heart untouched and untransformed.

Only Jesus can transform your heart and change your story. It's really that simple! That is why, by listening to the multitudes who have approached me with their stories, I can clearly hear and see the unique, memorable, and awe-inspiring details of stories that have been born out of a faith in God's grace. These stories show that you too can *change your story.* These stories are powerful because they center on an Audience of One: *Jesus Christ*.

ONLY JESUS CAN TRANSFORM YOUR HEART AND CHANGE YOUR STORY.

Maybe you don't believe you need to change your story, but I am sure you know someone who does. Yet, so many people who want change don't even know where to begin. Therefore, I trust you will allow these pages to speak to you as the apostle Paul spoke, "Boldly as I ought to speak . . ." (Ephesians 6:20, NKJV). with sincerity and yet without sensationalism. This I've experienced: Every change of story is a miracle in motion, and God is not done with any of us! How can I say this? Because Jesus Christ is the same yesterday, today, and forever (Hebrews 13:8, NKJV). What God has accomplished in someone's yesterday, He can do in everyone's today, and in anyone's tomorrow. This opens the door of hope to anyone wanting to change his or her story. God is limitless. He doesn't play favorites. He works in everyone with an unconditional love. But the big key is giving Him your "permission" and your trust. You must believe and have faith in Him. It's that simple.

Let me detail why I believe anyone can experience a change of story.

1. Everybody has a story.

Our lives tell a story. Every story has a beginning, a middle, and an ending. Our stories are defined by a set of experiences and encounters, both positive and negative.

2. Everybody's story is important to God.

Whether someone has a personal relationship with God or not does not diminish the unconditional love the Heavenly Father has for every person on His created planet. Even if someone says, "I don't believe in God," that doesn't stop God from believing in that person! Why, you may ask? Because every person is important to God. Thus, so is his or her story.

3. Not everyone has the story they want.

Every person likes and even welcomes the idea of change. Unfortunately, the overwhelming majority of people silently believe it's just not possible. Will Rogers once said, "People change, but not much." People desire change, but too many feel powerless to make it happen. But Jesus looks at us and says, "With man this is impossible, but with God all things are possible" (Matthew 19:26 NIV).

4. Jesus is the Story Changer.

Solomon once said, "Change is the way of life." My Pastor, Cesar Castellanos, once told me, "If I change, everything changes." Jesus is the master key to changing anybody's story, regardless of the past, present, or what an individual thinks about the future. Jesus came to Earth as the living embodiment of God's love. He's just looking for someone's permission to demonstrate that love.

In short, every "change of story" must begin with trusting His promises. Your change of story journey will be exciting. The results will be what I call "Ah-mazing!" It's time to begin your "Change My Story Journey." It's time to do as God instructed Abraham, "Now lift up your eyes and look from the place where you are, northward and southward and eastward and westward; for all the land which you see, I will give it to you and to your descendants forever" (Genesis 13:14-15 NASB).

Everywhere I go, I remind people . . .

> God knows where you are.
> God knows where you need to be.
> And only God knows how to get you there.

I pray that as you read this book, the Holy Spirit will work in you as God changes your story. I pray that your life will be all it can be, and that you will be equipped and empowered to reach the world around you.

> **MY PRAYER:** I ask, in Jesus' name, that you may be filled with the knowledge of His will in all wisdom and spiritual understanding.
>
> I pray that as He changes your story, by faith in His grace, that you would walk worthy of the Lord, fully pleasing Him, being fruitful in every good work and increasing in the knowledge of God. I pray that you will be strengthened with all might, according to His glorious power. May God give you patience and joy. May what is written here be words in season, to awaken hearts, as we live out our change of story.
>
> In Jesus' name, amen.

Now, let's begin our change-of-story journey.

CHANGE YOUR STORY

Do you believe I can do this?

—JESUS

1

A Change for the Better

I want to tell you something about God. God, who is Omniscient. Omnipotent. Omnipresent. The Creator of the universe. This God is deeply invested in the story of your life. He really is. Your life story fascinates Him.

Maybe the story of your life has not been what you once dreamed it would be. Right now, you might be frustrated, confused, disappointed, and discouraged about your story. Frankly, you may not be too sure if you even care about it anymore.

Well, let me tell you a powerful, life-changing, and undeniable truth: God cares about your story.

You might think that last sentence defies logic. But logic, as wonderful as it is, is completely limited when it comes to comprehending God's love for you and His plan for your life. God responds to our faith, not on the basis of our analysis of the situation. And the negative circumstances that may currently threaten and overwhelm us are trivial to Him.

God alone knows what your life, your story, was designed to be. God has changed countless lives. He can do the same for you. Why? Because His promises are infallible. In addition to that, His love for you is limitless—and that's where His desire to change your story begins.

Your Heavenly Father knows the way to change your story. As much as we *think* we understand God and His ways, we really don't. The breadth, width, depth, and height of His unconditional love are simply beyond comprehension. It's in a category humanly inconceivable yet tangibly life-changing.

Today, without being sensational, you can set in motion the miracle you need to change your story. What's that miracle, you may ask? **Permission**. I realize you may struggle with this, thinking that if God wasn't so busy with "other important things" He could somehow turn on the faucet and pour out the blessing of change you've been longing for. (Somebody's been watching too much television.)

No, you must give Him permission. Your faith in Him releases the Godly forces that will empower you and change your story. Faith is a very deliberate force. Your faith in Him is what will make you whole and, thus, change your story. Throughout the gospels, Jesus emphasizes the importance of people's faith in

God to receive breakthrough. Your faith is what gives God the permission to change your story.

I am writing this book because I want the God who loves you unconditionally to have permission to work His limitless power in your life. Your life can be a masterpiece. Even if things are not going well for you right now, it's not too late to change. There is still time because God is always on time. He's always ready. The question is, "Will you give Him permission?"

My hope is that the pages that follow carry God's blessing and anointing, so that readers just like you can see their stories changed by His grace and mercy. I trust that you, or somebody you know, will sense God's threefold cord that can change your story: faith, hope, and love. As Pastor Cesar Castellanos once told me, "Learn to look at people and your situation through the eyes of faith—it will change everything."

Let's go back to the quote that began this chapter: ***Do you believe I can do this?*** That's what Jesus said to two blind men who followed Him into Nazareth. (See Matthew Chapter 9 for the whole story.) How they answered the question would make all the difference in their world. Jesus wasn't asking them for deep theology. He didn't want the opinion of the ruling religious leaders of the day. He simply wanted to hear what these two men believed.

Jesus said, *"Do you believe I can really do this?"* When Jesus asks us a question, it's not because He doesn't know the answer. He doesn't need a confidence-booster. He knew exactly why He was asking the question.

Jesus knew exactly who He was, why He had come, and what He could do in that moment—if a show of faith would give Him permission.

Jesus' question to you today is similar to the one posed to the blind men 2,000 years ago: *"Do you truly BELIEVE I can change your story?"* I highlighted the word "believe" in the previous sentence, because belief releases permission.

BELIEF RELEASES PERMISSION.

Let's give God permission to change our stories. Let's watch what happens when we do.

When I think about people whose lives have taken amazing turns, I think about Matthew. Let's meet him and hear his story:

> *"As Jesus was walking along, he saw a man named Matthew sitting at his tax collector's booth. 'Follow me, and be my disciple.' Jesus said to him, so Matthew got up and followed Him"* (Matthew 9:9 NLT).

Wow, what a verse!

"Really?" you might be saying. "It sounds like a pretty simple story". Well, that depends on whether you are listening or not. Let's consider these words from Jesus:

> *"If you have ears, listen! And be sure to put into practice what you hear. The more you do this, the more you will understand what I tell you"* (Mark 4:22-24 TLB).

In other words, we should take heed **what** we hear—and not just what we hear but **how** we hear what we think we're hearing. You can hear something being said without *truly* hearing it! In other words, God can be speaking to us, but sometimes we are not listening to Him. We're not paying attention. The remedy is that we need to focus.

What if I were to tell you, "This is the perfect time to make the most powerful change you've been looking for"? You see, God is the Author of time and seasons. Time does not define God. God has defined time. The Bible says 1,000 years is as a day with God, and a day with God is as 1,000 years. God neither sleeps nor slumbers—because not only does He not need to, but because time does not define God! Here's what God is saying to Matthew: ***It's Your Time!*** It's time for your turnaround. It's time for your change. It's time for your salvation.

You see, faith in God releases God. It gives God permission to move into your situation and change your times and seasons.

That's why I say to you what Jesus was saying to Matthew: "It's your time!"

It's time for salvation. Time for deliverance. Time for healing. Time for that breakthrough. It's time for joy, for peace.

I understand that it can be hard to believe, "It's my time." Things can be so messy in our lives that we say, "It cannot possibly be my time. Everything in my life is going wrong! How can I hope to change my story now?"

If this sounds like you, I have good news: God doesn't wait for things to be perfect in your life, and life doesn't always feel good or right. God meets you right in the middle of your biggest mess and says, "It's time to step out of that mud! It's time to step out of your depression and step into joy! Step into the new life I have for you!"

Of course, the opposite can also be true. You might feel you are at the top of your game. You don't need God to do anything new, because "status quo" is working just great for you. You see, sometimes people get so used to misery that, instead of trying to get set free from it, they nurse it or rehearse it, but they never change it. That's not God's best!

This brings us back to Matthew. Here was a man at the top of his game. His status quo condition was good enough, as far as he was concerned. He was a wealthy tax collector. He had prestige, position, popularity, and power. He was prosperous. In fact, to some degree, he was enviable.

He was surrounded by yes-men. He threw and attended lavish parties. He had it all going on.

From a distance, we look at Matthew and say, "Wow! That guy has his act together. He has an influential, high-paying job, and the money seems to be rolling in. He has a prestigious title. He's known around town. He's society's high roller. He lives in the nicest neighborhood."

But as we get closer to Matthew, we find him to be an empty, broken man. A man miserable and despised. Matthew was a Jewish tax collector, and he worked for the Roman Empire. That meant Matthew's job was to collect money from his own people and hand it over to the Romans—the oppressors and despisers of Israel. So, he was viewed as a traitor. The people of Israel hated him.

What's more, tax collectors were known to be cheaters. They'd skim money off the top before turning it over to the Roman Empire. That's how some could afford a lavish lifestyle.

Now here's the "Wow Factor" in the story. The Bible says Jesus is walking along and He truly "saw" Matthew. Yes, Jesus physically saw Matthew, but what He actually *saw* was beyond what others could see. Jesus saw Matthew's heart.

He sees that Matthew is a hollow shell of a man. He knows

Matthew is hurting and alone and miserable—distrusted and rejected by his own people. In character, Matthew had become mean-spirited, a calculating man with a cold heart, even toward his own people. He was lonely. He had lackeys and hangers-on, but no true friends.

It's no accident that Jesus crosses Matthew's path. Nothing in the Bible is happenstance. It's a lesson to all who have ears to hear—like you and me. Jesus' time on earth was valuable, precious, and limited. He was on earth as a man for only 33 ½ years, and only 3 ½ years in ministry. Jesus' encounter with Matthew is destined. He speaks to this hurting man who is pretending to have it all together. He says, "It's time. Time for you to step out of that mess and step into something greater. *Follow Me and be My disciple.*"

I can only imagine how stunned Matthew was. No one, except the Roman Empire, ever dared speak to Matthew that way. But there was something about Jesus' words. They were bold, confident, and filled with authority. Yet they were also compelling, compassionate, and genuinely caring. There was no bribe or ulterior motive. There were no false promises, just a captivating invitation that filled Matthew's heart.

Jesus didn't offer Matthew a book deal. He didn't say, "Listen, if you follow Me, I'll give you the best book deal ever. I'm thinking of writing something that will be called 'The Gospel' and it will be in the New Testament! I'll make you famous. Everyone will know the name Matthew!"

No. Jesus' message to Matthew was much simpler. He was giving Matthew an opportunity: "Matthew, it's your time."

You may ask, "Time for what?" ***Time to change Matthew's story!***

And that is my message, again, to you: It's your time. The Author of all time is saying, "It's time to do new things, plow new ground, and step into a new light."

It's time to walk in God's best for you.

With all my heart, I want to encourage you: Do not miss your time! When God comes to you, please don't say, "I'm not sure I am ready. Let me think about this."

If you do this, you could miss a wonderful opportunity to change your story.

Let me show you how important God's visitation is, why this book emphasizes God's message, ***"It's your time to change your story"***—and why you don't want to miss this invitation.

YES, GOD IS A GOD OF SECOND CHANCES, AND THIRD CHANCES, AND BEYOND. HOWEVER, THAT DOES NOT MEAN THAT THE SAME OPPORTUNITY YOU HAVE RIGHT NOW WILL STILL BE AVAILABLE IF YOU DELAY.

Let's explore this concept in more detail, with another story about Jesus.

In Luke 19, we find Jesus approaching the city of Jerusalem and weeping. "Eternal peace was within your reach," He laments, "and you turned it down . . . and now it is too late. Your enemies will pile up earth against your walls and encircle you and close in on you, and crush you to the ground . . . for you have rejected the opportunity God offered you" (Luke 19:42-44 TLB).

Please note that Jesus is weeping here over a missed opportunity. He is not saying, "Serves you right!" No, He says, "Those things that are broken in your life, I can heal. I can make whole what has been shattered in pieces. If only you would realize that I alone am The One who can bring peace into your life."

Tragically, sometimes the peace we need can be hidden from our eyes. Jesus goes on to explain why those lives in Jerusalem will not experience *the change of story* that He alone can cause in their lives when He says, "You did not know **the time** of your visitation" (Luke 19:44 ESV).

Jesus said, "You did not know your . . . what?" *The time!* Jesus was crying over the people, and they didn't see it, didn't get it—what time it was.

What was possibly going through their minds? Maybe it was something like, "Jesus, I don't like your timing. I need to think this over. Besides, I'm good enough. My life isn't in really bad shape."

Or maybe they were saying, "You don't understand how long I've been like this—what I've been through. My situation is just impossible. Nobody can help me. I've accepted this as my lot in life."

If this sounds like you, and you feel your life is an unchangeable mess, then I submit to you: *It's your time!* God doesn't want you to wallow in that mess anymore. He's come to visit you and assure you, "I don't want you to be confused. I don't want you to hurt. I don't want you to be depressed. I don't want you to be poor. I don't want you to be discouraged. But I do want to take you out of this bad season of your life and take you into a new season. I do want to make your story better than it has ever been!"

Wherever you are in life, it's your time to decide. Jesus didn't speak to Matthew at his convenience, but He did speak to him at the *right time!* Matthew's change of story hinged on one thing—his decision to get up and follow Jesus, or stay where he was. But Matthew decided right. He chose to get up and leave his big-money, high-powered career. He realized, "It's my time to follow Jesus. It's time to step into something new. It's time to change my story! I don't know exactly where the road will go, but I will follow Jesus no matter what."

Matthew knew it was time, but how many people miss their time? How many people think they are smarter than God?

That they have it all figured out? God's timing is always better than ours!

Yes, God is a God of second chances, and third chances, and beyond. However, that does not mean that the same opportunity you have right now will still be available if you delay.

Opportunity can pass us by, leaving us filled with regret. God's timing is always perfect. He knows our lives better than we do. He knows things about us that we do not know. We just have to be willing to trust Him with all of our heart, lean not to our own understanding, in all our ways acknowledge Him . . . and be not wise in our own eyes. (See Proverbs 3:5-7 NKJV.)

Be like Matthew. Seize the moment and step into God's best for your life. Once you decide to step into His time frame by faith, your life will never be the same. It's not a leap in the dark; but it will be a stretch of your faith.

DECIDING TO STEP INTO GOD'S TIME FRAME IS NOT A LEAP IN THE DARK; IT'S A STRETCH OF YOUR FAITH.

Say to yourself, "It's my time."

Jesus is saying, "The day of salvation is here." I believe some people reading this book have never made a clear, purposeful decision to follow Jesus Christ. If this sounds like you, if you are unsure about where you stand, I am speaking especially to you right now. If you have one foot in and one foot out, it's your time! Be like Matthew. Hear and obey Jesus' call: "Follow me." Take that first step.

Imagine for a moment a game of baseball. You can't get to second base until you get to first base. It might seem like a small step, but small steps of faith in God always lead to giant results in life.

You can change your story. God knows that your life is an amazing story. You might not see anything amazing about your life right now, especially in light of past defeats or failures. Perhaps you have tried really hard, only to end up (in your opinion) as one giant flop.

Hey, we've all been there, me included. But I have good news. To fail is not our identity. It's an event. It's impossible to succeed if you're afraid of stepping out. The good news is that there is no failure in God, as long as you don't give up on the story of your life. Let's do what Matthew did. He didn't give up! You shouldn't give up either. It's your time!

2

Jesus, the Story Changer

D o you ever feel like a stranger in your own life story? Or, do you feel stuck? Have you ever asked, "How did my life story ever get so out of control?" Maybe you asked because you'd like to move forward, but at the same time you ask, "Where do I start?"

You know your story needs to change, like Matthew's in the previous chapter, but how do you make that happen?

I have good news: Jesus is the Story Changer! God has a plan for every person's story, and you're no exception! You are important. Your story is important. He wants to be fully invested in your story, along with you. How is this possible? Well, the Bible tells us that we are to "look unto Jesus, the Author and the Finisher of our faith" (See Hebrews 12:2 NKJV). So what does an author do? An author writes stories. The dictionary defines an author as an originator or creator. God Himself is the Author and Creator of life. And He's not done writing your story! That's right. The Bible encourages us that rewriting, improving, and expanding our stories is all within the scope of His strength. Paul wrote, "It is God Who effectually works in you ... creating in you the power and the desire. ..." (Philippians 2:13 AMPC).

God alone has the power to change a person's story. Only He can rewrite the story of the most impossible situation and make it possible. Let me help you understand that Jesus is the Story Changer by looking at the example of David.

Let's consider the story of David, the Old Testament king (and giant-slayer). David's life was anointed and blessed by God, above his older brothers. Favor and power were upon him. God raised up one of the mightiest kings the nation of Israel had ever seen. To this day, David is remembered and celebrated. Yet, talk about somebody who blew it, someone who seemed to disregard everything God had done for him!

But something happened to David, something that will encourage the saddest of hearts. In his later years, David's life was sometimes filled with turmoil. He cheated on his wife. He orchestrated the murder of an innocent man. He had strained relationships with his children. He lied.

And then something happened. As David described it, "God made my life complete when I placed all the pieces before him ...

God rewrote the text of my life when I opened the book of my heart. . . . ." (2 Samuel 22:21, 25 MSG). This Scripture helps us not only define God's unconditional love, but also shows how He wants to be understood *as a Story Changer.*

God can change any life story, no matter the person or the circumstances. He alone has this kind of power.

I like the way the apostle Paul says, "Your very lives are a letter that anyone can read just by looking at you. Christ himself wrote it—not with ink, but with God's living Spirit; not chiseled into stone, but carved into human lives. . . ." (2 Corinthians 3:3: MSG).

> **"GOD REWROTE THE TEXT OF MY LIFE WHEN I OPENED THE BOOK OF MY HEART. . . ."**
>
> 2 SAMUEL 22:21, THE MESSAGE

Think about that. Every day, people are reading our lives. That can sound like good news or bad news. After all, not everybody is living the story he or she wants to live. The good news is that God can change our stories. When we feel like we're withering on the vine, He can love us back to life.

God does not give up on us. He does not condemn us. He shows us mercy. Jesus came to this planet to change our stories. He changed my story. He changed it by His grace and power. He wants to do the same for you. I love stories of redemption. I remember after prayer one day, I sensed the Lord say, "I can change the story of a city by changing the story of one person at a time!" That phrase has echoed in my heart ever since, because it reveals the power of one changed life. The difference, impact, and influence one life can make. Now everywhere I go, I tell people: "God can change the story of a city by changing the story of one person at a time." Anybody can be that one person. God is ready anytime! Why do I believe this? Because each person really is important. One person can change the story of a city.

I know so many people who have been told, "There's no hope for you." Sometimes these people were telling *themselves* this bad news.

And then I saw God rewrite the story of their lives.

TO JESUS, THERE ARE NO INSIGNIFICANT STORIES, BECAUSE THERE ARE NO INSIGNIFICANT PEOPLE ON PLANET EARTH.

I love these stories. Stories of redemption and God's mercy. Stories of God rebuilding lives, remaking lives. God wins back lost hearts. God repairs broken hearts. God breathes life back into dying hearts. He restores lost hope.

You are not stuck in your story. Not with Jesus. He gets us unstuck every time. All of us. To Him, there are no insignificant stories, because there are no insignificant people on Planet Earth.

Sometimes we want to write ourselves off. We think, "I am so unworthy. I don't deserve anything good."

I know I thought that way.

But God responds with an amazing outpouring of mercy and compassion.

How amazing?

Well, let me introduce you to a man who felt his story was over. Chapter after chapter, things were only getting worse, until he encountered Jesus, the story changer. This is how he tells his story:

> "Hello, my name is Paul Kahale-Miner. I was born and raised on Oahu, in the state of Hawaii, and I was brought up in the church. My definition of being a Christian was just going to church every Sunday. Trouble started when I was 10 years old. My friend used to steal beers from his father and bring them down to the beach. We'd build a bonfire and start drinking, until we were so drunk we would just spin around and laugh. We thought it was fun. So we just continued to do it over and over, until we got introduced to cocaine. When we did the cocaine, we would gag, so to clear our throats we would drink more beer. It just was a vicious cycle. Every time we would drink, we needed cocaine, and every time we did cocaine, we needed to drink. At the time I thought it was fun, but looking back I was just living a lie after a lie after a lie. This went on for about 15 years."

"I got married and went through some difficulties because of the drugs and alcohol. We got divorced. We have three children together. We went to court and by some miracle, God gave me my kids. So I decided to move to the Big Island (another island in the state of Hawaii) to give them a better life. It dawned on me that in my house I wanted my kids to serve the Lord. But it wasn't until I got remarried and started living a comfortable life that I started going back to the same old thing: drugs and alcohol. Then I got introduced to crystal meth. Did that for 10 years. That's when my second marriage started to fall apart. When you get sick and tired of being sick and tired, it's when your heart opens. It turns your whole life upside down, inside out. It got so bad that my second wife, Kalei, left me. With her gone, and my kids in boarding school, I was left alone. Then my brother-in-law introduced me to a church called Word of Life, because he knew I needed help. He invited me to a weekend event they were having, called an Encounter. I didn't know what an Encounter was but I said, 'Why not?'

"It was there that I met Chauncey Pang, one of the assistant pastors at Word of Life. I believe that God brought this man into my life to help change my story. Meanwhile, Kalei had been praying that God would bring a mentor in my life, someone strong enough to make me sit down and listen, and love me back to life.

"Pastor Chauncey told me, 'I love you, because God loves you.' That's when God started turning my life around. Pastor Chauncey took me under his wing and helped me to see how Jesus could rewrite the story of my life. As years went on, he kept in close contact with me, calling me up and asking me how I was doing.

"For the next 10 years, Kalei and I flew to Honolulu from Kona to attend Word of Life Christian Center as often as possible. Why? Because I am learning to live my life story according to God's Word. He removed my desire for alcohol, cocaine, and meth. Word of Life has really helped me put my life back together. Thank You, Jesus, for this church. I am learning to be a better leader in my family, and beyond. I'm now a small-group leader to 12 committed men. When I see the changes in their lives, it touches my life. And, I am part of the team that opened a new church campus for Word of Life in Kona. Being a part of Word of Life Kona has been a blessing to our family and friends. Life is a great thing that we have the opportunity to do. And it's not just 'doing life.' It's having life in your living. It's a blessing to do life together with my wife. That's the greatest thing ever for a married couple.

"Like David, God rewrote the text of my life when I opened the book of my heart."

Isn't that a great story? It's a story of how prayer *works*. A story of how God can bring people into our lives, to change things for the better. As you reflect on Paul's story, I am going to ask you to consider three things.

First, to change your story, you must refuse to abandon the fight, "The Good Fight of Faith" (1 Tim. 6:12). (I'm not talking about fighting against people here.) Paul Kahale-Miner didn't give up, even when the drugs and the drinking sank their hooks into him again, later in his life. Some battles must be fought more than once to win. We must persevere.

I often like to say that the Bible reveals "God as a God of War, the Bible as a Book of Battles, and the Christian life as a Good Fight of Faith." Recall the words of the apostle Paul: "I have fought the good fight. . . ." (2 Timothy 4:7 NKJV).

Every fight requires an opponent. Sometimes the opponent is familiar, like the alcohol and drug addiction in Paul Kahale-Miner's story. However, I want to encourage you in a fight against a foe you might not know, but one that's very real.

The apostle Paul spoke of such foes in his letter to the Ephesians:

> *"Put on the full armor of God, so that you can take your stand against the devil's schemes. For our struggle is not against flesh and blood, but against the rulers, against the authorities, against the powers of this dark world and against the spiritual forces of evil in the heavenly realms. Therefore put on the full armor of God, so that when the day of evil comes, you may be able to stand your ground, and after you have done everything, to stand" (Ephesians 6:11-13 NIV).*

What these spirits or negative influences attempt to do is to contain you. I call it "The Spirit of Containment." You might be wondering, "What is the Spirit of Containment"? Let's think about that last word. To contain means to limit something, to hold it back or hinder its effect.

It can be unpleasant to think about enemies like this, but the Bible warns us that we indeed have an adversary who is working against us. Jesus said, "I will build my church; and all the powers of hell shall not prevail against it" (Matthew 16:18 TLB).

Yes, our victory is assured by Jesus, but this does not mean that our enemy won't try to prevail.

In this fight, I want you to understand that you are a lethal weapon for God's Kingdom. You might not feel this way, but you are important. You are significant.

This brings us back to The Spirit of Containment. Our enemy wants to contain us or fence us in. He'll try to get us to live a smaller life, even though in Christ our lives aren't small. It's what I refer to as living a reduced version life, a shrink-wrapped life, or a downsized life based on how you feel or what unbiblically based religion has falsely told you. When you are in Christ, you are not religious; you are a new creation. A believer is no longer contained or fenced in by the senses. We are to walk by faith not by sight. Let me help you understand what the Holy Spirit reveals through Paul the apostle, in his letter to the Corinthians.

Now remember, the Corinthian church was made up of born again, Spirit filled, church going believers. Yet Paul says to them. "Dear, dear Corinthians, I can't tell you how much I long for you to enter this wide-open, spacious life. We didn't fence you in. The smallness you feel comes from within you. Your lives aren't small, but you're living them in a small way. I'm speaking as plainly as I can and with great affection. Open up your lives. Live openly and expansively!" (2 Corinthians 6:11-13 MSG).

What Paul is telling this church is powerful!

These people don't see that they are living their life stories in a small way. Their stories are not actually small, but that's how they are being played out. You see, our adversary wants you and me to accept limits of small living. This is not how God designed us to live.

I don't want to insult anyone's intelligence, but it's worth considering what the word "small" truly means. The dictionary offers definitions like "minor in influence, power, and importance" or "lacking in strength."

Paul was reminding his Corinthian readers, "Your lives aren't small or minor in influence. They don't lack strength, and they are not trivial. But you are living as if you are small!"

What Paul said then, I assure you now: *"Your life is not small."*

"Well," you might counter, "you don't understand what's going on in my life!"

Your life is not small.

"Hold on—you don't know the hardships I am facing."

Your life is not small.

"You don't know what the doctors have told me."

Your life is not small.

Please understand—Jesus did not go to the cross and defeat the devil by being raised on the third day so that we would continue to live small. He paid a staggering price to eliminate our sins and set us free. He gave us abundant life. He calls out, "I have come to give you life more abundantly" (John 10:10).

The adversary wants to cut your story short, get you to believe in a small shrink-wrapped mentality. He wants to downsize your dreams. He would love it if your story doesn't have an epic climax and happy ending. Is the Holy Spirit saying to you or someone you know: "The smallness you feel comes from within you"?

Is the Spirit saying, "Your lives aren't small, but you're living them in a small way"?

Paul, by the power of the Holy Spirit, wants to ensure that none of us lives a small life—whether we realize it or not. He urges us to be open to the things of God. I don't believe that anything in the Bible is there merely to entertain us. The Bible was created to help us find our destinies and fulfill our life's purpose.

> IS GOD'S SPIRIT SAYING TO YOU, "YOUR LIFE ISN'T SMALL, BUT YOU'RE LIVING IT IN A SMALL WAY"?

Some of the people in Corinth didn't think they were missing anything. Paul said, "Really? Are you remembering to fight the Good Fight of the Faith? And, if you don't know what you are fighting for, what is the point of your story?"

God's promises are not fairy dust that He sprinkles on us just so we can have a Tinker Bell Moment and say, "Hey, I feel good!"

Our stories do not work that way. We don't stand around, waiting for "Bless Me Dust." We walk by faith. We don't compromise. We don't tolerate small living when God paid such a big price to set us free. Remember always that what you tolerate, you authorize to stay in your life.

WHAT YOU TOLERATE, YOU AUTHORIZE TO STAY IN YOUR LIFE.

It's sad what some people authorize to stay in their lives. Is there something destructive, or something limiting, that you are authorizing to stay in your life?

God created us. We didn't create Him. And the Bible is like an owner's manual for a car. It tells us how things are supposed to function. Without God's Word, we don't know how to fulfill our purpose. We don't know how to treat people, how to love people, or how to forgive people.

God knows where you are, and He knows where you need to be. Only God knows how to get you there—to get you from the page you are stuck on to the pages ahead. That is what He did for Paul Kahale-Miner; that's what He can do for you.

So that's the number-one thing I want you to consider: Remember to "Fight the Good Fight of Faith.

Second, to change your story, you must never forget the

"Power of the Red Door." I love this. Say the words: "The Power of the Red Door."

In a house, a door separates one space from another. It can separate the living room from the kitchen, the kitchen from the bathroom, and so on.

On a larger scale, a door separates the inside from the outside.

When I shared this message with my church, I had a big red door brought on the stage to use as an illustration.

"This door," I explained to my congregation, "leads from one experience to another experience. Jesus said, 'I am the door. If anyone enters by Me, he will be saved. He will enter and find green pastures.'" (See John 10:9.) Moreover, Jesus adds that on one side of the door, we are lost, unredeemed. We are all twisted up in negative stuff. But one day, we pass through the doorway called Jesus.

He is the way, the truth, and the life. No one can approach God the Father except through Jesus. (See John 14:6.) When we pass through this door, we step into green pastures, which symbolize the blessing of God's light, mercy, peace, joy, and love.

It's like passing from a dark chapter to a chapter with hope.

Jesus is the door to eternal life. He is a door open to everybody. Once, I had a story on the wrong side of the door, but then I walked through my own personal Red Door.

Say that again: The Red Door.

When we walk through that door—bam! Jesus changes our story. He says, "You have the right to change your story, to live an abundant life, because of the blood I shed. You have a right to change your life. You don't have to live as a failure. You were lost, but now you are found. (See Luke 15:24.) Heaven was not your ultimate home. Now it is."

The color red should remind us that we have been bought with a price. In Ephesians 1:7, Paul tells us, "In Christ we are set free by the blood of his death, and so we have forgiveness of sins. How rich is God's grace" (NCV). I just love that verse!

I also love what Peter says: "He paid with Christ's sacred blood, you know. He died like an unblemished, sacrificial lamb" (1 Peter 1:18-19 MSG).

Later, the Bible states: "And they overcame him by the blood of the Lamb and by the word of their testimony. . . ." (Revelation 12:11 NKJV).

In the Old Testament, we see the story of the children of Israel—God's precious people. They had their own Red Door Day. They were in bondage and cried out to God. So He sent a deliverer named Moses. God told Moses, "Pharaoh is being very stubborn. I am going to clear some things up for him. I am going to send an angel of death, but whoever follows My instructions will receive My blessings and protection. The angel of death will pass by them."

God's people were instructed to place the blood of a lamb (symbolizing Jesus' future sacrifice) on the lintel and doorposts of their homes.

What does the lintel and the doorpost represent? You might have guessed it: The cross that would bear our Savior more than 1,000 years later.

So, when God is talking to Moses and the Israelites, He is also talking about how you and I are going to be delivered and set free. How we are going to be protected. As the Bible says, we overcome by the Blood of the Lamb and by the word of our testimony. (See Revelation 12:11.) This word of our testimony is not in our natural talents or even our spiritual gifts. Our testimony is rooted in the Power of the Blood. This power was marked from the days of the Old Testament, and it was confirmed in the New Testament.

Jesus rose from the dead to set us free!

But . . .

Given this amazing truth, why do some people walk through the Red Door, while others stay stuck, living fenced-in lives? Maybe you know people like this.

The Corinthians, the target of Paul's letter, were people who walked through the Red Door. They had been born again and filled with the Holy Spirit. But they were living as if little demon imps had put fences around them.

Some of us behave like those Corinthians. We attend church regularly, but we live small lives. As Paul said, "Your lives are not small, but you're living them in a small way."

Why is this?

Stuff happens.

Yes, our lives are full of stuff, full of circumstances and crises. Full of the wrong kind of people, who stuff our brains with all kinds of junk. God wants you to un-brain yourself of this stuff. Un-brain? Is that even a word? Nonetheless, I think you know what I mean!

Have you ever looked at someone and said, "That person has so much potential. But why is he so insecure? Why is he such a storm of emotions—twisted up one day and broken down the next?"

We can't always see what is going on inside people. We all have our struggles. But I am here to tell you: Your story is greater than you realize.

We are the Church, and the Church is so much more than a building. The Church is God's people. The gates of hell shall not prevail against us. But our adversary will *try* to prevail, because he knows that you and I are lethal weapons. In his mind, we must be stopped.

I promise you that you are important. The enemy knows that. He knows the power that is yours in Christ Jesus. He knows the Power of the Red Door. The enemy knows you can help people see the truth and live out that truth in their daily lives. You have spiritual gifts. Those gifts have our enemy scared. This is no time to be limited or contained!

Let me show you how a person can get fenced in.

Let's assume I have a problem with unforgiveness. I am aware of the problem, but I have never really done anything about it. So unforgiveness is part of my thinking. I might think that my unforgiveness is not fencing me in. In reality, however, it's doing something even worse: It is slowly burying me!

We have all made mistakes. Those mistakes must be dealt with. Otherwise, they worm their way into our hearts and minds and influence the way we think, act, and speak. Past mistakes also intimidate you every time you try to step into new territory. That's why we can go to church but not be changed. We hang on to the baggage of the past—stuff God says it's time to get rid of.

Of course, not everyone carries the same baggage. For some, it's discouragement. For others, it's disappointment. And what about the baggage brought on some of us by parents or other authority figures?

Whatever your "stuff," the Bible says it's time to renew your mind and avoid being conformed to the ways of the world. (See Romans 12:2.) The Bible says it's time to forgive people, to cleanse ourselves of negativity. We must guard our hearts with all diligence, for out of our hearts flow the forces of life. (See Proverbs 4:23.)

I want my story to be a force for good. Don't you?

I realize that some of you reading this book have experienced awful things. I encourage you to remember the power of the Red Door—the power of the Cross that sets us free. We are set free to forgive people, to be kind to people, to love people. Even if those people are acting unlovable, unforgiving, or just plain flaky.

We might have a reason to act in a certain way toward others, but we do not have an excuse. The Bible is our standard of behavior. Not our will, but God's will be done. (See Luke 22:42.)

I realize that what I am saying might sound like criticism. It's not. Paul did not criticize the Corinthians, and God's Holy Spirit is not here to berate us. That is not how He changes your story.

The Bible says we should speak encouragement to one another. We should lift people up. That is how Jesus did things. In that spirit, I am telling you that you have the power to let go of past mistakes. You can choose to get rid of negativity in your life. You can choose to let go of unforgiveness. You have the power to break the chains of fear.

Like Paul the apostle, I am encouraging you to, "Open your lives. Live an open and expansive life" (2 Corinthians 6:11-13 MSG).

Third, to change your story, we must never forget about the power of choice. Many people continue to live fenced in lives because they don't understand the power behind their own choices.

Paul the apostle wrote, "Only be careful that this power of choice (this permission and liberty to do as you please), which is yours, does not [somehow] become a hindrance. . . ." (1 Corinthians 8:9 AMPC).

You are not stuck. You always have a choice. In fact, God is telling us, "I call heaven and earth to witness against you today, that I have set before you life and death, the blessing and the curse. So choose life in order that you may live, you and your descendants," (Deut. 30:19 NASB).

You must exercise your power of choice by choosing not to stay where you are. You can change. You can get out. Where you are right now is not your final destination. But God will not make up your mind for you. It's your choice.

Making the right choices can change lives. It can reignite your passion and direction in life. God will always do His part, but we must do ours. Choose to move forward.

I understand the fears and the negativity. I understand the

disappointment. Reflect for a moment on Paul Kahale-Miner's story from earlier in this chapter.

That story is living proof of how we can overcome our obstacles by the Blood of the Lamb and the Word of God. We don't have to live oppressed, depressed, or defeated.

We stand before an Audience of One, the King of Kings and Lord of Lords. We have the power of choice. Let us use that power and allow God to guide us as we live big, not small.

Let's allow God to change our stories, for good.

3

The Cure for N.U.M.B.

Christian. What image comes to mind when you see or hear that word? I Googled the word "Christian" the other day and got more than 1.23 billion results. That would be a lot of reading. It would be quicker to visit the Wikipedia page or consult Webster's dictionary. Or, I'm sure I could ask Siri, "What is a Christian?" and she would have an answer.

Did you know that Christian appears only three times in the entire New Testament? And it's not used by a follower of Christ to describe him- or herself.

Here's something else that might surprise you: Of those three New Testament mentions of *Christian,* not one is used as a compliment. That's right. It was a derogatory term, at least at first. After the persecution of the church in Jerusalem, Christ's followers scattered in all directions. Some found a home in a place called Antioch, a Greek-speaking, Roman-minded city.

It had no church, but it had almost everything else you can imagine. (Antioch is located in modern-day Syria.) Some of the locals began to make fun of the newcomers, and "Christian" was one of the names they used. "Look," they would say, "there goes one of those Christians."

Did you know that a name so many of us are proud to bear today was once an insult?

However, those doing the mocking did take notice of the way the Christians lived. Their lifestyles differed in intriguing ways. They were loving and kind. They were people of character. Even the way they spoke was different. They faced cruelty and persecution with a quiet and humble dignity. Antioch's residents saw Christians handle adversity differently from other people.

And, of course, these Christians talked about Jesus all the time.

The Bible tells us that the disciples were first called Christians in Antioch. (See Acts 11:26.) The disciples launched a church. But they did not call themselves Christians As noted above, that was a label pinned on them by other people.

Later, Peter used the term, in reference to Christians being persecuted. He wrote, "However, if you suffer as a Christian, do not be ashamed, but praise God that you bear that name" (1 Peter 4:16 NIV).

The third time the word appears, the apostle Paul, a prisoner at the time, is defending himself before King Agrippa. The king says to Paul, "Do you think that in such a short time you can persuade me to be a Christian?" Paul replies, "Short time or long—I pray to God that not only you but all who are listening to me today may become what I am, except for these chains" (Acts 26:28-29 NIV).

Note that it's Agrippa, not Paul, who uses the word "Christian." *Disciple* was the key word in the early church. That's what Christ's followers called one another. Jesus' disciples lived powerful lives, without being extravagant or sensational. God's presence was very real in them. That's what I want us to realize now. Discipleship is the open door to living a transformed life, to experiencing a changed story.

We will learn more about discipleship later in this book.

Words like *disciple* and *Christian* are labels, of a sort. Labels can be positive or negative. When you buy a new gadget, it usually comes with lots of information. There is the owner's manual—which some people (me included) never read. Then there are the various labels. Some instruct us what to do, while others warn us what NOT to do.

Have you ever read a warning label and wondered, "Why

> DISCIPLESHIP IS THE OPEN DOOR TO LIVING A TRANSFORMED LIFE, TO EXPERIENCING A CHANGED STORY.

did the company have to include this warning? And then you realize that someone, somewhere, must have done exactly what the label warns against. In fact, because some of these labels are bright orange or screaming yellow, maybe more than a few "someones" made the same mistake.

Here are a few actual warning labels I have seen:

On a sunshade for a car's windshield: "Do not drive with sunshield in place."

On a hair dryer: "Do not use while sleeping."

On a microwave oven: "Do not use for drying pets."

On a box of rat poison: "Warning: This product has been found to cause cancer in laboratory mice."

On a bottle of children's cough syrup: "Do not drive or operate heavy machinery while taking this medication."

On a child's Superman costume: "Wearing of this garment does not enable you to fly."

Here's one from a box of hammers: "May be harmful if swallowed."

Last one—on a bottle of sleeping pills: "May cause drowsiness."

My congregation always gets a good laugh when I read these

from the pulpit. We should be thankful for warning labels, but it's a little scary that companies feel like they have to warn people not to swallow hammers.

In life, the Bible is our user's manual. It contains the warnings we should heed if we want to live fulfilling lives. Many of the Bible's directives seem like good common sense, but take a look at those warning labels above. Clearly, people do not always exercise common sense.

The Bible provides wise rules for life, so that people won't invent their own ideas of what a Christian is, or what a disciple is.

There are two things I believe are true of every person on earth:

1. We all want to be happy.
2. We are all going to die.

From the time we are born, we are on a quest to discover happiness, to live a meaningful life. As we grow and mature, we find direction in life. Those of us who decide to follow Christ understand that He is at the center of everything. He helps us live lives full of meaning and purpose. He brings us true happiness, which we can experience all the days of our lives. The Bible provides the guidance we need to lead fulfilling lives.

Now, let's consider point number 2: We are all going to die.

I don't mean for this to be morbid. I recently presided over a funeral, and it was wonderful to be there. Yes, I was sad for a family's loss. But this individual had led a life of impact. I saw the effects of this life on generations of people, beyond just the immediate family. The chapel was overflowing with people.

I ministered to these people from the Word of God. I reminded them that God has prepared mansions for all of us. I reminded them of Jesus' words, "If it were not so, I would have told you. . . ." (John 14:2 KJV).

It was a meaningful service, because this man had lived his life as a true disciple. He was a Christian in the best sense of the word. He lived out a story that mattered, one that impacted so many people.

He had lived a transformed life. This is the kind of life God wants all of us to live. He wants to transform our marriages, our friendships, our faith, our finances, our physical health, and more. He doesn't want us to merely talk about or read about transformation. He wants us to experience it. He wants to be our story-changer.

Jesus is often called the Great Physician, for good reason. Psalms 147:3 says, "He heals the brokenhearted and binds up their wounds" (NIV).

In the book of Exodus, God reassures Moses that He is Jehovah Rapha, that is, the God who heals. The Hebrew word Rapha is very powerful. It refers to more than just healing someone of a disease. It means completely restoring and reviving that person. Think of an expert mechanic taking a classic car and lovingly restoring it to pristine condition, better than the day it left the factory.

In Acts 10:38, Peter testifies about Jesus, proclaiming, "Then Jesus arrived from Nazareth, anointed by God with the Holy Spirit, ready for action. He went through the country helping people and healing everyone who was beaten down by the Devil" (MSG). The New International Version translates the verse this way: "God anointed Jesus of Nazareth with the Holy Spirit and power, and how he went around doing good and healing all who were under the power of the devil because God was with him."

Let's not miss one word of this wonderful verse. Jesus was anointed by God to do good! God wants to do good in the lives of His disciples. He wants to heal you and restore you. He wants to be relevant in every aspect of life.

At this point in the book, I hope you believe that God wants to do good in your life. But here is a tough question for you: Is there someone in your life who you cannot even imagine becoming a follower of Christ? Someone who is hard-hearted and resists you whenever you try to talk about spiritual matters? Maybe you feel this person has crossed so far over into the Dark Side that there is no returning.

Perhaps you think of yourself this way. Do you ever tell yourself, "I'm not qualified to be healed by Jesus or to be one of His disciples. I know what I am like inside. I do not deserve to have my story changed."

A lot of people talk to themselves this way. But I am here to assure you that Jesus came to heal people just like this. He came to transform lives and make disciples. His promises hold true for you, no matter who you are or what you might have done. You can have a transformed life right now. I'm not talking about when you get to heaven someday. I am talking about your life on Planet Earth! I am talking about the "right now" of your story.

I encourage you to live with this truth. Jesus is your healer. He wants to restore you and rewrite your story. He does not want you to live in the place called N.U.M.B.

What is N.U.M.B.? Trust me: N.U.M.B. is a real place, populated by Christians and non-Christians. The scary thing is that many people do not even realize they are living here. They tolerate living N.U.M.B. and don't ask questions. Half the time, they don't even realize what is happening to them because they can't "feel it" or "sense it." They're "numb."

We arrive at N.U.M.B. because of the way we've been conditioned to think and act, as well as life's encounters and experiences that have repeatedly bombarded our lives without any resistance. That's why the Bible warns, "Do not conform to the pattern of this world, but be transformed by the renewing of your mind" (Romans 12:2 NIV). If we fail to have our minds transformed, we can live on auto-pilot. We make choices and adopt behaviors because we follow the patterns of others, or because we take the path of least resistance. Others follow a particular lifestyle because it's part of their cultural background.

Jesus shares a different message: "Don't live numb. Uncondition yourself! Wake up!"

What, exactly, is living N.U.M.B.? I will spell it out for you.

The "N" in N.UM.B. stands for Negativity. It's no accident that I will devote an entire chapter (Chapter 10) to the dangers of living negative. Our world is full of critical, cynical people. Think of how much of today's social media is devoted to making fun of celebrities, politicians, religious groups, ethnic groups, and even common individuals who somehow end up on someone's "hit list." Cyber-bullying is a major problem in today's schools.

It's easy to get caught up in all the negativity. Could this be happening to you? How is your perspective on life? How do you feel about your own story? Do you find yourself saying, "Nothing ever works out for me"? Why should I even try to achieve something? I never succeed. In fact, no one in my family has ever succeeded."

That last statement is very telling. Some people seem to feel that negativity is inherited. Someone thinks, "My marriage isn't going to work out, because my parents divorced—and so did their parents."

Another says, "I'll never graduate from college, because no one in my family has ever earned a degree. We just don't have the intelligence or perseverance to get a degree."

The "U" in N.U.M.B. stands for Undecided. Do you know people who are undecided about their lives? Often, these people are uninterested, unmotivated, and uninspired as well. "UNs" often travel in packs. Undecided people don't lack intelligence. In fact, someone who is undecided can be thinking too much—without ever directing those thoughts and coming to an actual conclusion. It's like staying in college for eight years because you can't decide on a major.

On a spiritual level, people can hesitate to give every area of their lives to Christ. They hold back and hedge their bets. And they miss out on the blessings Jesus wants to offer. They miss the chance to make their stories full and vibrant. They get stuck in their stories because of indecision and uncertainty.

The "M" in N.U.M.B. stands for Mediocrity. So many people wind up living mediocre lives. They have lost their passion for life. Every day is routine and mundane. It's deceptively easy to slip into mediocrity, because there is so much unproductive routine in modern life. Many of us wake up at the same time every day, eat the same breakfast, take the same route to work, and do the same tasks over and over. It doesn't mean that certain everyday habits aren't good, but that certain everyday habits aren't changed, improved upon, or eliminated. A mediocre life will ultimately lead to a miserable life. It's as if we're mindless—we're not giving what we're doing any thought or attention. We simply wake up every day and follow the path of pointless pursuit.

At home, you can fall into a routine with your spouse and your kids. You can find yourself behaving out of habit, rather than desire—the desire to be a good husband or wife. The desire to teach children how to follow Jesus. The desire to do some good in the world. Some people think that mediocrity is an age thing. We get older, and we run out of steam. But it's not an age thing; it's a spiritual thing! No one should settle for mediocre, lukewarm, passive, or status quo. No one should bump along without thinking!

> **"I WILL PRAISE YOU, FOR I AM FEARFULLY AND WONDERFULLY MADE; MARVELOUS ARE YOUR WORKS, AND THAT MY SOUL KNOWS VERY WELL."**
>
> PSALMS 139:14 NKJV

As the psalmist says, "I will praise You, for I am fearfully and wonderfully made; marvelous are Your works, and that my soul knows very well" (Psalms 139:14 NKJV).

Isaiah puts it this way: "Yet you, LORD, are our Father. We

are the clay, you are the potter; we are all the work of your hand" (Isaiah 64:8 NIV).

Remember this always: You are the product of God's creative action. You have been shaped and formed into a person of great worth. You are anything but mediocre.

Finally, the "B" in N.U.M.B. stands for Brokenhearted. So many people today live with broken hearts. It's a place where people have been defeated, disappointed, and discouraged. Such setbacks push us into a certain mentality after a while. It affects the way we perceive everything. It's like looking at the world with dirty glasses. Your entire perspective is tainted.

Here is something else I have noticed about brokenhearted people: They don't want their hearts broken ever again. This makes them reluctant to make new relationships, or to let current friends and family get too close. The result is a numb and closed-off existence.

The dictionary definition of numb includes phrases like "a lack of sensitivity." If your emotional nerve endings are insensitive, you cannot feel the love in your marriage or sense the joy in your Christian walk. Your story is limited. You are living N.U.M.B.

That's why the Bible says that we must guard our hearts. (See Proverbs 4:23 and Philippians 4:7.)

We have already met a man with a classic case of living

N.U.M.B. His name is Matthew, and we explored much of his story back in Chapter 1.

At this point in the book, I want to explore a bit more of Matthew's story, to remind us what we can learn from it. In Matthew's case, Jesus was like the Great Physician Who made a house call. He didn't wait for Matthew to come to Him. Jesus never wasted any time. In the 33 years that He walked the Earth, everything was calculated. He didn't waste His days or His words.

Speaking of house calls, I grew up on Garden Street on the east side of Santa Barbara. My sister got sick one time, and my mom called the doctor. The doctor actually made a house call. Can you imagine that happening today? That was the first and last house call our family ever received.

Today's doctors are very, very busy. It's hard to get an appointment at their offices. It's clear that their schedules are packed. The waiting room is always crowded. Some offices charge you a penalty if you miss an appointment. It's like an assembly line. There is no room for a glitch in the process.

So that one house call really sticks in my memory. That personal touch really made a difference for my sister and our whole family.

Matthew received his personal house call from Jesus, because the Great Physician knew he was suffering from a disease called N.U.M.B. Jesus saw Matthew from the inside out.

He saw who Matthew truly was, not the façade he was trying to present.

As you might remember from Chapter 1, Matthew was a Jewish tax collector—working for Rome, Israel's oppressor. His own people viewed him as a heartless traitor. He was like a New Testament Benedict Arnold.

Further, Matthew was skimming money from the taxes he collected. That's how he bankrolled his lavish lifestyle.

Matthew was considered a parasite. Everywhere he went, he was scorned and sworn at. It's possible that the Jews might have even tried to stone him.

No wonder Matthew was living a N.U.M.B. life. He had all the trappings of wealth, but inside he was a storm of misery.

Like Matthew, some of us construct this restrictive world for ourselves and wonder, "How do I get out of this?" Matthew was miserable, but he didn't dare show it. He had to project power and confidence.

Are you a little like Matthew? Are you miserable but hiding it? Are you surrounded by people, but lonely deep inside? Do you feel that you have no true friends? Jesus wants to make a house call to you. He doesn't want you to feel helpless and hopeless.

Here's an interesting historical fact: Tax collectors like Matthew often operated from a high perch. They could see all the merchants—who was bringing in the most money, who was selling contraband, who was taking bribes, and so on. But inside, Matthew felt low. He hated the way his story was playing out.

Then Jesus approaches. Jesus looks at Matthew and sees directly into his soul. That's what the Bible tells us about our Lord. People notice the outward stuff, but God looks into the heart. (See 1 Samuel 16:7.)

I am here to tell you that Jesus has His eyes fixed on you right now. He sees into your soul. There is nothing you could tell Him that would shock Him. He already knows your story well.

After making contact with Matthew, Jesus offers him a most unusual invitation: "Follow Me and be My disciple. . . ." (Matthew 9:9 NLT.)

This raises a question: Who are you following in your life? And I don't mean following on Twitter or any other social media. In Greek, "to follow" means to walk on the same road. As we live out our stories, Jesus wants us to walk the same road with Him.

"Follow me," is a command. You cannot be a disciple without obedience.

To Matthew, that command was astounding. Here was Jesus, a Jewish teacher, reaching out to a Jewish traitor, a renegade. As a rule, no Jew wanted anything to do with Matthew and his kind.

So when Jesus spoke, Matthew heard, "Matthew, I want to be your friend, and I want you to be my friend."

It is also important to realize that Jesus doesn't speak of Matthew's past. He doesn't scold him for his dishonesty and disloyalty to his own people. He doesn't call him a scum or a sinner. He doesn't say, "How could you!?" He says, "Be my friend, and I will be yours."

Jesus behaved this way because he is the Great Physician, Who saw someone who desperately needed healing. He knew it was time for a house call.

Jesus is the same today. We might feel unworthy of Jesus' friendship and love. What have we done to deserve *that*?

But Jesus says, "Follow Me. Let Me rewrite the text of your life."

Are you following Jesus? Are you His friend? Or do you keep Him at a distance? Do you feel like you are living N.U.M.B., trapped in a life from which there seems to be no escape? Are you stuck in your story? God is not criticizing you. He doesn't want to use your past as a club to beat you over the head. He doesn't want to shame you in front of your peers.

Instead, He is calling you to Himself. I pray you will be like Matthew. I pray you will respond. Because, my friends, that is what life is all about—a personal encounter with Jesus. Jesus wants to meet you face to face and author your story.

Jesus wants to bring you healing. He wants to be your friend. He wants you to follow Him and be His disciple. If you are willing to do this, Jesus will change the story of your life. He wants you to live a story that is beyond anything you can hope or imagine.

With those thoughts in mind, let's close this chapter in prayer:

> Father, we come to You, and we are so thankful for the lives You have given us. How amazing is every person reading this book! What wonderful stories are in store for them! I truly mean that!
>
> We thank You for the healing in Jesus' name. As Jesus made a house call to Matthew, may we all understand that He still makes house calls today. Jesus knocks on the doors of our hearts. He invites us, "Follow Me. Be My disciple."
>
> How amazing that You want to be our friend, and You want us to be Yours. I pray that You will speak to every heart. Heal us, mend us, and fix us. You are the Great Physician. We need Your healing.
>
> I know that some people reading this book might be unsure where they stand with You. They might respect You. Perhaps they grew up learning about You. But they don't have a close and loving

relationship with You. Before they close the pages of this book, I ask You to heal those hearts—all those areas that need Your healing touch.

Father, we know that Your salvation is without limits. May those who need that salvation sense the knock on the doors of their hearts. May they know that the Great Physician is there, ready to work healing.

I know that there are other readers who are just hanging on by a thread. It's been too long since they have truly felt Your presence. They have lost the confidence in Christ that they once had. They want to get it back. They need You to write a comeback into their stories. May You heal their every wound, mend their broken hearts. I thank You in advance for the supernatural work You can do in these lives, if only they will open the book of their hearts.

Right now, I extend my hand in faith to each and every one of these people. I ask You for a tangible work, a real work of Your Holy Spirit. Guard every heart. There are wonderful things You want to do in these lives. Things beyond all imagination or understanding.

We are grateful that You do not come to criticize. You come to renew and restore. You invite us to walk in a relationship with You. Release the Holy Spirit in our lives to transform our hearts and renew us. Change us with Your love, mercy, and grace.

I pray all these things in Jesus' name,

Amen.

4

Getting Unstuck

I once heard a life-changing question, one I'd like to share with you now. When I heard it, I wrestled with its simplicity—and its complexity. I wasn't sure if I should just ignore the question or accept its challenge, a very personal challenge to me as a pastor, leader, father, husband, dreamer, and visionary.

The question: Where will you be one year from now?

That one simple question challenged my faith, my focus, and my future. I confess that, time and again, I tried to dismiss the question. I was a very busy man with a hectic schedule. Didn't I have more pressing matters to wrestle with? But this is why most people get stuck in their story. They're either too caught up with their present circumstances, or trapped in their past. Without having a vision for the future, our past and present can have too much power over our lives.

This question kept tugging on my heart, compelling me to offer some kind of response. As time rolled on, I had to confess that I was trying to avoid the question out of fear—the fear that I didn't really have an answer! How could one simple question be so intimidating?

Have you ever wrestled with this question—or something similar to it? I bet you have. We all know that "one year from now" will inevitably come to pass. It doesn't matter who you are, what color your skin is, how old you are, or how much (or how little) money you make. We all face that very real moment called "One Year from Now."

No matter how good or bad things are, most of us want to change the stories of our lives in some way. We need God to change our stories. And if we want God to change things, we must be willing to take what I call The Faith Challenge. I have learned that we cannot conquer what we do not confront. And we can't confront what we do not identify. Our question, "Where will you be one year from now?" prompts us to identify where we are so that we can move forward to where God wants us to be. I often tell my church, "God knows where you are, and He knows where He wants you to be. And only God knows how to get you there."

With these thoughts in mind, I want you to picture something with me: Your life, one year from right now. As we have seen, each life is a story. Imagine the year ahead as your story's next chapter.

Because you are reading a book titled "Change Your Story," I understand that you would like to look to your future with optimism and hope. But that might be hard to do right now.

Please, I want you to believe what I am going to tell you right now: The year ahead will be your best year yet. And this isn't one of those generic "Be positive!" proclamations. I am being honest with you, and the Bible will back me up. In the pages still ahead, I will prove this to you: Your best is absolutely, unequivocally, and undeniably yet to come. There is no doubt in my mind or heart.

Your life is a story, an amazing story. Granted, you might not see anything amazing about your life right now. Perhaps you are holding on to past defeats and past failures. You've tried hard, only to end up feeling stuck. We've all been there. The good news is that there is no failure in God; therefore, He is the only person who can get you unstuck, as long as you don't give up on the story of your life!

"Nah," you might respond. "You're just saying that because that's what pastors are supposed to say. Or maybe you think it will sell more books." I understand the skepticism. I know how people think. But here is the truth: God has great things for you, just ahead. You might not be able to see them right now, but your best days are yet to come.

GOD HAS GREAT THINGS FOR YOU, JUST AHEAD. YOU MIGHT NOT BE ABLE TO SEE THEM RIGHT NOW, BUT YOUR BEST DAYS ARE YET TO COME.

Try saying that: "My best days are yet to come."

How did those words feel?

Forced?

Insincere?

Doubtful?

Maybe you couldn't bring yourself to say them. Maybe something is holding you back. The Bible tells us we need to forget the stuff behind us and reach forward to the things that lie ahead. (See Philippians 3:13.) This is such wise advice. Because until we let go of the things behind us—those things that hold us back and weigh us down—we cannot grab hold of what is ahead.

In other words, to move ahead in your story, you need to turn the pages forward. You need to make the decisions and take the actions that empower you to grow closer to Jesus, to go deeper in your relationship with Him. The Apostle Paul said, "You received Christ Jesus, the Master; now live in him. You're deeply rooted in him. You're well-constructed upon him" (Colossians 2:7 MSG).

This book is about you and the decisions you will make, but it is also about God, Who has already made a decision on your behalf. God sent His Son, Jesus, to the cross to pay for your sins, and mine too. He sealed the decision with the Resurrection. He calls out to you, "You have the right to abundant life in my Son, Jesus Christ."

You have the right to an amazing, fulfilling story. If the story you have is not the story you want, it's time to change your story!

Because of Jesus, you are on the verge of a breakthrough. It's time to move forward!

In Philippians 3, the apostle Paul says we are to be "forgetting those things which are behind and reaching forward to those things which are ahead" (Philippians 3:13 NKJV).

Another version of the Bible puts it this way: "Forgetting the past and looking forward to what lies ahead" (TLB).

This is what I am asking you to do right now: Leave the past behind and move ahead in your story. The year ahead of you is a year to go further and grow deeper. Yes, I realize that your life story might contain all kinds of struggles—struggles of the spirit, body, and mind. Financial challenges. Relationships that are painful.

We have all made mistakes, seen failure, and experienced loss. That doesn't mean God doesn't have a future for us. That doesn't mean He doesn't want our stories to turn out amazing.

That is why it is so vital to move forward. You see, the past can fence us in. Past mistakes can make us feel so guilty or discouraged that we accept living a contained life. It puzzles our minds and paralyzes our spirits. We can't picture God fulfilling His promises in our lives. Every picture that comes to mind is dark and dreary. You look at the story of your life and say, "This story cannot end well." But it can and will if you'll step out and trust Him with the story He has for your life. The prophet Jeremiah reported, "'For I know the plans I have for you,' declares the LORD, 'plans to prosper you and not to harm you, plans to give you hope and a future'" (Jeremiah 29:11 NIV). That's why it's important to forget the past and look forward to what lies ahead: His plans for your life; His hope; and a bright, restored, and stronger future!

As I am privileged to minister here in Hawaii at Word of Life Christian Center, I often look out over the church each week and I know that there's not a single person who is not somehow, in some way, working on his or her life story. Even if someone is facing conflicts—and every story has some level of conflict—I know that God is bigger than any conflict.

Consider the following conflict, a conflict involving an entire community: The Old Testament book of Second Kings tells of the true story of the Samaritans. In the 9th century B.C., these Samaritans were attacked by a group of people called Syrians. The Syrians surrounded their city and cut off all of their supplies. The Samaritans gave up hope. They hung their heads and waited to starve to death. Things were desperate. How desperate? In the throes of extreme hunger and panic, some mothers ate their own children.

I feel bad even bringing this up, but it is true. And if God can change a story this awful, He can change any story!

As the Samaritans were trapped in a mire of despair, God sent a prophet named Elisha. Elisha spoke up boldly, saying, essentially, "In just 24 hours from right now, things are going to change. Your lives are going to be radically different. You are starving now, but soon food will be plentiful . . . and cost next to nothing!"

Imagine being one of those Samaritans, amid the sickness, starvation, and cannibalism. What would you have thought of Elisha's message?

We know what one of them thought. An officer of the Samaritan king was not impressed by Elisha's prophecy. He summoned Elisha and asked him, "Look, even if the LORD should open the floodgates of the heavens, could this happen?" (2 Kings 7:2 NIV).

In other words, this officer decided to disbelieve in the supernatural. Every day, we do the same thing. We decide what to believe about God and what He can do in our lives.

If you're struggling right now, you might be thinking, "Here we go again. I'm back in the same mess as before. There is no hope for me."

But I am here to tell you that things *are* different this time. This isn't going to be the same old story. You stand at the doorway of a life breakthrough! I understand the scars and the haunting memories of the past. These memories tie up our faith. They keep us stuck, unable to press on to our future. That's why I encourage you right now: Do not let your past punish your future! Remember the story of Matthew, the story of Paul Kahale-Miner.

Now, let's return to our story of Elisha and the Samaritans: That Samaritan officer, who thinks he is oh-so-smart, doubts that God is going to do something amazing for His people. He doesn't think they will break free from their captors. He thinks they are going to starve.

DON'T LET YOUR PAST PUNISH YOUR FUTURE!

Listen to what Elisha tells him: "You will see it with your own eyes . . . but you shall not eat any of it" (2 Kings 7:2 NIV).

What does that mean, exactly? Elisha is saying, "God is going to do just what He said He would do, but you are not going to be part of the breakthrough, because you have decided not to believe."

What Elisha said 3,000 years ago, I am saying to you today, my friend. The year ahead will be a breakthrough year for you! In one year from now, things will be radically different for you. Radically, positively different!

As I write these words, I know how many readers will respond: "I'd like to believe all of this, but you don't know my history. You don't know how I am feeling inside."

I know this because I have heard words like these from people in my church. I am here to tell you what I tell them: "I don't know your history, but I do know about your future! I am here to tell you that there's a God Who has your future in the palm of His hand!" He is here to change your story. He understands that everything might not be picture-perfect right now, but He has a vision to change your story, to make it better, to make it different. You are not stuck. You don't have to live in a rut. You don't have to live in pain all your life. You don't have to live hurt. You don't have to live diseased. You don't have to live broken.

It's time for you to break through. Don't blow it at the border of your breakthrough. You might not realize just how close you are to turning the page to the best part of your life story! The most significant part, the most joyous, the most amazing! If I were sharing these words in my church right now, I would be shouting, "Come on, somebody say Amen!"

Of course, I realize that sometimes it's hard to say "Amen." That brings us back to the Samaritans again. They were not saying "Amen" to Elisha and his bold prophecy about their future. They were prisoners. Their food supply was cut off. Their supply to everything good was cut off. They were a mess. But God had made a decision about them. He had already decided to love them unconditionally, to forgive them fully for anything they had done wrong. To set them free, in every sense of the word. He wanted to love them back to life. He wants to love YOU back to life. This life, for you, is found in Christ. And you must decide to live this life. You have to decide to walk by faith in Jesus. He supplies the life; we supply the decision to walk in it. We have seen what can happen when we make the right decision. And we'll see more real-life examples in the pages ahead.

I encourage you with all of my heart: Stay faithful, no matter what your past looks like. No matter what your present looks like. Your best is yet to come. Forget the stuff that is behind you. Reach forward to what is ahead of you.

And what is ahead of you? A great life. The best days of the story of your life. It's time to turn the pages forward.

With this thought in mind, I'd like to share what Elisha did for the Samaritans. He called forth four lepers. You probably know about leprosy. Leprosy means your life is falling apart, sometimes literally!

These lepers had stories with no hope. As I've said, "Everybody has a story, but not every story that everybody has is a story that everybody wants." Here, they were, outcast from the rest of the people. Nobody cared about them. They lamented, "Why do we sit here till we die?" They had decided to give up. They believed they could make no kind of difference for themselves or anyone else.

They were wrong.

Encouraged by God's prophet Elisha, they made one simple decision. They rose up. They decided they were not going to sit around and wait to die. They went into the Syrians' camp to see if they could get some food if they surrendered. They figured that if their enemies killed them, at least death would be quick.

They entered the encampment at dawn. They were amazed at what they found.

You see, the night before, God had raised a ruckus.

He miraculously created the clatter of chariots, the thunder of hoofbeats, and the roar of a great army attacking.

The Syrians were sure they were being attacked by their enemies, the Hittites and the Egyptians. They fled on foot, leaving everything behind, including their food, silver, gold, horses, and donkeys.

The lepers reported what they found, and the Samaritans rushed in to plunder the camp, an abandoned camp full of riches. Elisha's prophecy came true. Two gallons of flour and four gallons of barley were made available for about one dollar.

As for that officer, as he tried to control traffic at the city gate, he was trampled by the crowds. He saw the riches Elisha predicted, but he did not share in them.

Here's what God teaches us through this story. The people made a great breakthrough because four very sick, deeply hurting people made one decision. One decision transformed a city and saved lives.

Imagine what one decision can do for you and those you love. Decide to turn the page and make the year ahead one to remember.

5

Breaking Through

Across the world, many people view America as "the land of opportunity." For them, it's a place for a fresh start or continued growth in a career or field of study. It's one way they can move forward and find new breakthroughs for their life stories. And for any breakthrough, there must be faith in God's way of doing and being right. This reminds me of what happened in the Old Testament book of Numbers, chapter 13. God has brought the children of Israel out of Egypt to the border of a land called Canaan, a land "flowing with milk and honey" (Numbers 13:27). They have traveled for almost two weeks, and now these people find themselves standing at a borderline. But this border represents something more than just a natural border that separates two territories. Symbolically and spiritually, it represents the border of the breakthrough. Now, all they have to do is . . . cross over!

Crossing over means leaving the past and stepping into the new. (The new was God's plan—His best for Israel.) To prepare for this breakthrough into new life, Moses sends 12 spies to investigate the land. Twelve leaders venture into this new territory, but ten of them return with a negative report. Why negative? Because there were obstacles to be conquered. It was going to require change, a different way of thinking. Joyce Meyer has often said, "New level, new devil!" (Sometimes a person's way of thinking can be so tainted by negative past experiences that a view of a better tomorrow is actually problematic.)

Back to the story: Only two spies, Joshua and Caleb, came back with a positive report. These two spies understood God's plan. They were looking at the God-possibilities. They had faith in God's plan for their lives. They had confidence that in their God, all things were possible!! Joshua and Caleb were surprised that the people decided to go with the majority. They were stunned that their peers were ready to believe the doubters instead of God. And unfortunately, they were about to blow it at the border of their breakthrough! Imagine that! After coming so far, and after they saw miracle after miracle happening before their eyes as proof that God was leading and guiding them. You may ask, "How was this possible?" It's called *choice.*

The Israelites are about to make a choice that will move their story in a wrong direction. They are about to do what so many people have done—follow the majority. But little do they know that following majority rule, the popular direction, or the fashionable thing will cost them their destiny and keep them from experiencing God's best. Their story is about to take a wrong turn.

Question: What is holding you back from moving forward in your story? Following majority rule? Trying to fit in with the popular people? Or is it a broken relationship? A huge financial mistake?

Please believe me: We have all made mistakes. Even the successful businesspeople you know, the successful ministers or entertainers. There is not one person, in any field, who has not experienced failure. The only difference between success and failure is that some view failure as their identity. They get stuck because they live in their past mistakes.

So this is what I hope for you. Turn the page. Move *forward*, in Jesus' name.

Of course, history is filled with famous names. To paraphrase a video I heard from Hillsong Church, "from the tenacious to the notorious, the religious to the

> WE HAVE ALL MADE MISTAKES... EVEN THE SUCCESSFUL PEOPLE YOU KNOW. THE ONLY DIFFERENCE BETWEEN SUCCESS AND FAILURE IS THAT SOME PEOPLE REFUSE TO LIVE IN THEIR PAST MISTAKES. THAT IS WHAT I HOPE FOR YOU. TURN THE PAGE. MOVE FORWARD.

sacrilegious." What images cross the window of your mind when you hear the following names?

Socrates. Churchill. Mussolini. Mandela. Einstein. Hitler.

As Hillsong notes, names are pregnant with meaning. What do you feel down deep in your soul when you hear the name Jesus?

Is He a mystery to you?

A holy man who fought the powers that be so slaves could become kings?

Is He a deity who chose to endure mortality so that we could enjoy eternity?

Jesus. The name that opens blind eyes and deaf ears. It cures the sick. No other name carries such importance.

Some say Jesus' miracles are just fairy tales, but if that is so, why do millions of people gather in Jesus' name, many of them putting their lives on the line to do so?

I have come to this conclusion: **There is no other name like Jesus!** The Bible says every knee shall bow and every tongue shall confess that Jesus is Lord of things in Heaven, on earth, and under the earth. (See Philippians 2:10.)

The name of Jesus is powerful, unstoppable, undeniable, and unchangeable and will allow you to not only get to the border of your breakthrough but literally to **break through** whatever is keeping you from God's best.

There's an encouraging passage in the Old Testament that will give you insight into what God has for you on the other side of your breakthrough. It's found in Deuteronomy 11:8: "Therefore you shall keep every commandment which I command you today, that you may be strong, and go in and possess the land which you *cross over* to possess" (NKJV).

Tell yourself, "I am crossing over."

Deuteronomy 11 verse 9 goes on to say, "and that you may prolong your days in the land which the LORD swore to give your fathers, to them and their descendants, 'a land flowing with milk and honey.'"

Here again, like those Old Testament people, we are at the border of our breakthrough!

The next verses add, "For the land which you go to possess is not like the land of Egypt from which you have come. . . ."

In other words, God wants to take us someplace new—a "land of hills and valleys which drinks water from the rain of heaven, a land for which the Lord, your God, cares; the eyes of the Lord your God are always on it, from the beginning of the year to the very end of the year" (Deuteronomy 11:10-12).

We are like those people from the Old Testament. If we are willing to cross over, God will crown the coming year with His goodness. He will lead us on paths that drip with abundance. (See Psalms 65:11.) In the story that began this chapter, Caleb and Joshua were ultimately rewarded for their faith in God's promises. Why? Because they chose to follow God and trust His promises for their future. The doubters suffered because of their lack of faith and hope in God's plan and purpose for their lives. Solomon said, "There is a way that seems right to a man, But its end is the way of death" (Proverbs 14:12 NKJV). (Death is this context means defeat, failure, no productivity, and emptiness.)

A similar choice is ours today. We must decide to live in a new way to experience our breakthrough. Each of us must say, "I am going to go further this year. I am going to grow deeper in Christ. I am going to put God first in my life. I am going to let the Holy Spirit work in my soul."

When we are willing to surrender to God, phenomenal things can happen in our lives.

The Bible urges us, "Honor the LORD with your possessions, And with the firstfruits of all your increase; So your barns will be filled with plenty, And your vats will overflow with new wine" (Proverbs 3:9-10 NKJV).

Your "barns" are your bank accounts, your piggy banks, or even the cash stashed under your mattress. The "new wine" in this Scripture refers to the Holy Spirit. (This is an important fact to remember whenever you read this term in the Bible.)

And don't all of us want God's Holy Spirit to bring an

overflow of new things to us in the year ahead? God has so much He wants to reveal to you by His Spirit!

As we approach the end of this chapter, this is my prayer:

Father, in the name of Jesus, we come before You. Thank You for Your promise that we can go further in our lives and grow deeper in You. We can grow in spirit, soul, and body. That we don't have to settle for just knowing there's a promised land, or that there's a borderline separating where we are and where You desire us to be. Father, thank You for Your revelation that we can break through any border and change our story in the name of Jesus.

Father, I know that for some people reading this book right now, You are beyond imagination. Thankfully, we do not have to live by our imaginations. We can live by the truth of Your Word. We don't have to be prisoners of our emotions. We are free to live by Your principles and promises. How wonderful it is that we don't have to figure out everything! We have only to decide to live out our Change of Story!

As I write this prayer, I know so many people are at the border of a breakthrough! I pray that everyone reading these words will decide to believe in the power of following You in the year ahead. Let them all experience the works of the Holy Spirit, the promises of Your Word, and the outcomes of decisions made in faith and obedience.

I thank You in advance that, one year from now, we will look back and see how far we have come, how much we have grown, and how we have prospered. For this, we will give You all of the glory, honor, and praise. Amen.

Now it's your turn. Here is a responsive reading for you. Please read the words aloud, and with all sincerity and hope:

Heavenly Father, in the name of Jesus,

I dedicate and devote my life to the power of one year with Jesus Christ.

One year with Jesus at the center of everything I decide to do in my life.

I thank You that You are the God of forgiveness, the God of restoration, salvation, and deliverance.

Forgive me for my past. I choose to forget that past.

I choose to reach forward to everything You have in store for my life.

Thank You for the future and the hope You have for me, my family, and my other loved ones.

I am blessed that Jesus is the Lord of my life.

In His name I pray. Amen.

6

Rewriting Your Story

I want you to imagine your change of story one year from now! Do you believe that if God puts His hand on something, He's going to bless it?

How we answer this question is vital if we truly want the next chapter in our stories and the next year in our lives to be the best one yet.

What could your life look like if you devoted one year to God? As you imagine the answer to this question, remember that God exists beyond our concept of time frames. To Him, a day is like 1,000 years. Conversely, 1,000 years is like a day. (See 2 Peter 3:8.) That's because God is the author of time. He is not limited by time, as we are. He uses the concept of time to help you and me understand what He is doing in the seasons of our lives.

He can change time. He brings fruits to bear at the appointed time, and He brings us into new seasons in our lives. As you are reading this book, God is doing a new thing in your life. He wants to take you to a new level in every area of your life—spirit, mind, body, finances, *everything*.

You can move forward in so many parts of your story: your marriage and family, your friendships, your career, and, of course, in the ministry work you do if you trust God to rewrite your story.

When I talk about "the power of one year" in this book, I am talking about the powerful things God can do in your life story if you will devote the year ahead to Him. He will do something amazing! And I should point out that God is not limited by one year or any time frame. He doesn't need a time limit to make a breakthrough happen, to make a miracle happen. I am using one year because there seems to be something about this particular time period. God mentions it continually throughout the Bible.

God's Word is filled with verses about "one year." Psalms 65:11 (NIV) says, "You crown the year with your bounty, and your carts overflow with abundance." Deuteronomy 11:11-12 proclaims, "But the land you are crossing the Jordan to take possession of is a land of mountains and valleys that drinks rain from heaven. It is a land the LORD your God cares for; the eyes of the LORD your God are continually on it from the beginning of the year to its end" (NIV).

Hosea 10:12 exhorts us, "Plow new ground for yourselves, plant righteousness, and reap the blessings that your devotion to me will produce. It is time for you to turn to me, your Lord, and I will come and pour out blessings upon you" (GNT).

When I read verses like these, I am certain that God is trying to give me something. He wants to get His blessings to me. He's not trying to get something from me. And couldn't we all do with a few more blessings in the year ahead?

This Scripture from Hosea packs four powerful statements that reveal to us the steps we need to take to allow God to rewrite our stories.

First, Hosea tells us to plow new ground.

The key word is new. God is a God of new things. If you are looking at your life right now and don't see the hope of anything new, of the possibility of a breakthrough in your story, you are not seeing your potential in God. Please believe me. God is asking you to plow new ground.

How do we do this? We're going to figure it out together right now. The first step is to understand the challenge that your Heavenly Father is putting before you. New ground is new territory in your life. It's like the next level on a job or the next grade in school. It's like a fresh, new chapter in your story. We leave the old and stagnant behind. We stop looking back at the past. We move forward, upward, to something new.

The year ahead promises something new for you, something for your best. And even if things have been good for you, God's going to unveil something better. He always takes us from glory to glory, from strength to strength. From faith to faith.

God wants you to do something you haven't done before. He wants to bring you new accomplishments, not accumulate more of the old ones. What is in store for you? Achievements beyond your planning or even your wildest imagination. The Bible promises us that God has good things in store for us—things we haven't even thought of!

IF YOU ALWAYS DO WHAT YOU'VE ALWAYS DONE, YOU'RE ALWAYS GOING TO HAVE NOTHING MORE THAN YOU HAVE RIGHT NOW.

The New Testament says it powerfully: "Now to Him who is able to do exceedingly abundantly above all that we ask or think, according to the power that works in us, to Him be glory in the church by Christ Jesus to all generations, forever and ever. Amen" (Ephesians 3:20-21 NKJV).

This is an amazing verse, but I would mislead you if I didn't point out the flip-side: If you always do what you've always done, you're always going to have nothing more than you have right now. Yes, what you have right now may not be bad. It might be pretty good. But it is less than all there is available for you!

That's why God urges us to plow new ground. Step into new

territory. There are things God wants to give you. You might not think these blessings or opportunities are for you. God is encouraging you, "Sure they are! This is my inheritance for you. My promise for you."

So, as we move on, we must remember that we cannot become what we need to be by remaining where we are.

At this point in our journey together, I want to ask you, "Where are you right now?"

It might be someplace good, someplace comfortable for you. You are satisfied. But are you where you *need* to be? Are you all you could be, should be?

These are important questions, because our God is a God of progress. In the discipleship process at our church, we strive to promote people's spiritual progress and their growing joy in believing in God. Progress is forward motion. It is not stagnant.

Did you know that the biblical Greek word for disciple (*mathetes*) refers to a student or apprentice? In ancient times, the term was often associated with people who were followers of a great religious leader or teacher. A disciple is a learner. Learning is all about progress. And one of the beauties of being a disciple is that you can be a learner at any age. You are never too old or too young to learn! You are never too young or too old to be a devoted follower of Jesus! This is why I can assure you that your best is yet to come. God always has something better for us, as we learn from Him and follow Him more closely. We plow new ground. We bear new fruit.

Now let's move on to the next part of our Hosea Scripture:

Second, Hosea tells us to plant righteousness.

Righteousness is an intriguing word. Let's look at Matthew 6:33, from the Amplified Bible, Classic Edition: "But seek (aim and strive after) first of all His kingdom and His righteousness (His way of doing and being right), and then all these things taken together will be given you besides."

So we see that righteousness is Jesus' way of doing and being right.

> YOU CANNOT BECOME WHAT YOU NEED TO BE BY REMAINING WHERE YOU ARE.

Now, sometimes we do things that we think are right, or we do things that other people say are right for us to do. But there's what we think, or what people think, and then there's what **God** thinks. That's why He says, "For My thoughts are not your thoughts, neither are your ways My ways, says the Lord" (Isaiah 55:8 AMPC).

So, when God instructs us to plant righteousness, He is asking us to make a commitment. A commitment to handle our marriage His way, to handle our finances His way, to handle our children His way, to handle *all* relationships His way, and to handle our thoughts His way. A commitment to His way is a commitment to live our lives according to God's Word, the Bible.

To do things God's way, we must be submitted to His wisdom and guidance. We cannot try to force our way into God's plan.

How many times do we insist on pushing our way, even though it's not working for us? It is so vital for us to understand that "planting righteousness" requires making firm decisions. We decide to speak God's words, not what bubbles out of our minds—without our truly thinking about what we are saying. We decide to walk by faith, not by our feelings, which can be manipulated by so many factors.

How many times has this happened to you: Someone cuts you off on the freeway. Your emotions boil over. You give into road rage, but that is not the way God wants you to respond. I encourage you to pause for a moment and examine your life. Which areas does God want you to work on? Does He want you to change the way you think about yourself? Does He want you to change the way you think about certain other people in your life? Maybe it's both of the above.

Are you clinging to thought patterns and behaviors that you need to change—behaviors you have been trying to justify?

For example:

> "I am rude and sarcastic to a co-worker because he is rude and sarcastic to me!"
>
> "I am giving my spouse the 'silent treatment' because that's what I always get."

Have you ever tried to justify something like this in your mind? These are the kinds of attitudes and behaviors God wants to get rid of. He wants to pull up the old weeds and plant something new and healthy, and righteous.

Third, Hosea tells us to devote ourselves.

Our Hosea 10:12 Scripture promises that we can "reap the blessings your devotion to me will produce" (GNT). Devotion to God will produce blessings in your life. When you choose to devote yourself to God and take your life in Him to the next level, He will be there to help you step up. He is asking for devotion from you. He is asking for your loyalty to Him and your enthusiasm and dedication. This will produce more good things in your life. Devotion is not drudgery. It's not a burden. Devotion is a joy!

Jesus was devoted to His Heavenly Father. He found joy in proclaiming God's goodness and grace.

DEVOTION IS NOT DRUDGERY. IT IS NOT A BURDEN. DEVOTION IS A JOY!

Jesus' disciples were devoted to Jesus. They boldly and joyously proclaimed the new life Jesus was offering. With a sense of urgency, they told everyone, "Your life can be radically different!"

Devotion. Let's consider that word further. Is there something you have not yet devoted to God—committed to Him? Is it your speech—the way you communicate? Are your words negative or sarcastic? Don't we all fall into this trap? We don't necessarily go around mocking people, but our words tear down, rather than build up.

Technically, we might not be sinning with our words, but they are not what they should be. Devoting our speech to God means changing how we talk, or text, or even tweet.

What about the way we think about ourselves or others? Do you have a friend or family member or co-worker who criticizes you all the time? Always judging you, analyzing you. And you think, "Who are you to judge me?"

However, we all need to understand that God loves that person who criticizes us—or whom we criticize. He loves these people unconditionally. And if God loves someone unconditionally, who are we to critique him or her? Who cares if that guy dresses weird? Who cares if that woman is socially awkward?

We don't need to be critical. Can't we be nicer people? What a novel concept for our life stories, right? What if we *devoted* ourselves to make a simple decision to be nicer people? One little adjustment could have a huge outcome!

I promise you that when you live your life devoted to God—when you are loyal to Him—you will walk more closely with Him. You will have better relationships with those around you. What you sow in your life will bring about a great harvest. And that is not all! When people see this harvest, they will take note.

They will listen to you as you share how God has changed your story for the better. More and more people will want to hear that story and be inspired by it! You can become a leader in your church and your community.

All of our stories are different, but all can inspire. We're all different in certain ways, but that's OK. God wants to work with you where you are in life, with *who* you are.

Here is a simple truth for you. Your devotion to God will produce blessings in your life. You will move forward to new territory, where the land is better, greater, and richer.

Again, I know that some reading these words right now are thinking, "Life's pretty good."

But let me tell you—you don't understand all God has for you. He is calling out to you: "I am ready to pour blessings upon you, if only you will devote yourself to Me."

Fourth, Hosea tells us it's time!

"It's time for you to turn to me, your Lord," our verse says. Some readers might be thinking, "Well, that part of the verse doesn't apply to me. I already go to church. I study my Bible all the time. I even go to a small group!"

If this sounds like you, I have a question: Have you truly turned everything over to the Lord? After all, we can get so caught up in the routine of regular church attendance and Bible study that we lose our sense of true *devotion*. We fall into going through the motions, checking off the items on our spiritual to-do lists. There is a huge difference between devotion and routine.

At this point, I need to be assertive and make sure you are hearing something you might be missing. When some believers hear, "It's time to turn to the Lord," they respond, "Yeah, yeah, I have already done that."

Who are you responding to when you say this? Your pastor? The people in your Bible study group? Yourself?

Or, are you saying this to the Lord? Can you honestly tell Him that you're at the highest possible level? Can you say before God, "My Christian walk is the best it's ever been, and I am not procrastinating about anything"?

Please understand me: I am not saying there are not great things going on in your life. I am simply saying that God has so much more for you. It's time to trust God to rewrite your story. Time is two things. Time is this moment, a moment in which you can decide to take your life to a new level. Don't procrastinate and risk missing that moment! Time might also be a new season in your life. God wants you to move forward into this new season! Do not delay. Turn the page on the calendar!

To enter this new season, we must decide. To paraphrase Proverbs 3:5-6, God is saying, "It's time for you to turn to Me.

To trust in Me with all your heart and lean not on your own understanding. Trust Me with your whole heart, and I will direct your paths."

Think about something with me: Are you walking a certain path—maybe it's a relationship path—and things are just not working out? If this sounds like you, whose path are you walking? You see, there is your path, and there is God's path. Just because you are a Christian, you cannot assume you are automatically walking God's path. It's not programmed into you, like GPS. We all must choose to walk God's path. We choose by trusting God and following Him. When we do this, He guides us. He says, "Turn this way"—even if a bunch of other people are turning in a different direction. You might say, "I want to follow the others."

God responds, "I understand, but I want you to go in a different direction. I am taking you where you need to go, not where others need to go. And not where you think you should go. It's time to decide to follow Me."

With all my heart, I encourage you: Decide to follow Christ. And decide right now. Don't delay! You have not reached your peak. The high point of your story is yet to be written. There might be very little that's wrong in your life. I am happy for you. But God has yet more. You might be unable to see more. That's OK. You do not have to see it. You just have to trust Him.

After all, Hebrews tells us that "faith is the substance of things hoped for, the evidence of things NOT seen" (Hebrews 11: 1 KJV, emphasis mine).

For others of you, the story is sadder. You feel you've hit a dead end. You are saying, "I cannot go further in my marriage" or "My career is stuck in quicksand. It's over. Time for me to quit."

God is saying, "No, it's not. You have no idea what I have in store for you. Devote yourself to Me. I want to bless every single area of your life. Your best is yet to come!"

Let me echo that as we end this chapter, and this book's first section. Your best is yet to come!

CHANGE
YOUR
STORY

Come, follow Me.

—JESUS

7

A Miracle in Motion

In the mid-11th Century B.C., God's chosen people, the Israelites, were being oppressed by the Midianites. They cried out to God, and He sent someone to help them.

But this was no ordinary "someone," as you're about to see.

As we pick up the story, an angel of the Lord visits a man named Gideon. Gideon is threshing wheat in a wine press—to hide it from the ruthless Midianites. (These wine presses were hewn from solid rock and stood about three feet tall.)

The word angel means, simply, "messenger." This angel has a message from God. He brings Gideon help and direction from heaven. A good disciple should be open to God's message.

Does Gideon take this message to heart, and set his miracle in motion? Or does he resist the change God is trying to bring to his story?

Let's keep in mind that the angel arrives for a one-on-one encounter with Gideon. This is significant. God is showing us that He cares about each of us as an individual. He wants a personal relationship. Of course, we must be open to God's messenger. If we allow the messenger, or the person discipling us, to speak into our lives and steer us back on course, great things can happen. Miraculous things can happen.

Like his fellow Israelites, Gideon had cried out to God about the cruel oppression of the Midianites. He asked the Story Changer to change this particular story.

When Gideon called out, God showed up. He sent an angel. This is another symbol for us: God will send someone to help when we ask.

In Gideon's case, it's an angel who assures him, "The LORD is with you, mighty warrior" (Judges 6:12 NIV).

Gideon's response? "Whoa, whoa!"

Well, not those literal words, but perhaps their Hebrew equivalent.

The point is . . . Gideon resists. He wonders, "If the LORD is with us, why has all this happened to us? [T]he LORD has abandoned us. . . ." (Judges 6:13 NIV.)

And why did Gideon resist? Because of his past. He had been suffering for the past seven years. He was so afraid the Midianites would steal his wheat that he was hiding it in the wine press. Wine presses were composed of two huge vats, where juice was extracted from grapes. Sometimes, the wine was made by people called treaders, who walked around and around in circles, crushing the grapes beneath their feet. (The grapes were crushed in one vat; the juice was collected in the other.) It's an apt picture of what the Israelites had been doing for seven years—walking in circles and going nowhere. And they felt like the life was being stomped out of them.

Do you ever feel like you're going in circles? Like you can't see the whole picture of the Christian life? You want to grow in your faith, in your story, but you're not sure how.

Take heart. We all feel this way sometimes. That's why the world needs disciples and those who will disciple them. For example, a hot-tempered person turns his life over to Jesus and has a born-again experience. Does everything change in an instant for him?

No. That fiery temper is still going to boil over from time to time. No one is perfect. I know that in today's culture, people want "instant everything," but real life doesn't happen like that.

Yes, Jesus instantly changes your heart, but, meanwhile, your flesh is freaking out. And your mind has to go through the process of being renewed. Gideon didn't understand this. That's why he questioned God's loyalty to His people. And that's why he didn't think the Midianites could be defeated.

You see, Gideon had a history. So he protested to the angel, "How can I save Israel? My clan is the weakest in Manasseh, and I am the least in my family" (Judges 6:15 NIV). He felt unworthy and powerless.

Gideon is so similar to many of us. Someone tells us, "You can live an abundant life. You can have peace and joy and prosperity and God's goodness!"

We respond, "You obviously don't know about me. You don't know about my past mistakes and failures. You don't know how all hell is breaking loose at my house!"

This is when we need to listen to the messenger and the message. God tells Gideon, "You don't see yourself the way I see you. Don't live trapped by your past. Be transformed by the renewing of your mind."

The moment Gideon cried out, God began to move in his life. However, Gideon's progress was slow. You might remember that he was the guy who kept looking for signs of God's favor (such as laying out a fleece). But in the end, Gideon and only 300 men defeated their enemies.

I am here to tell you that Gideon's story can be your story too. You're that one person who can make a huge difference. I realize you have reasons why you can't go forward. I urge you to take the apostle Paul's advice: Forget what is behind and strain toward what is ahead. (See Philippians 3:13.)

It was hard for Gideon to let go of the past. He struggled with the messenger's advice, at first. Eventually, he changed his entire nation. And it all began by changing his own thinking.

So it begins with you and me. We have the power to choose. We can stay put or move forward. We can choose to believe God and His words, or believe something else and go another way.

Let's go God's way. Being a disciple, a fully devoted follower of Christ, is a choice for something better. Gideon felt bad about his past, about his family reputation for weakness and insignificance. God saw him differently. He called Gideon a "mighty man of valor."

What I am going to say to you next, I say prophetically. That means I am saying it by the Spirit of God. I don't know what baggage you are carrying or what thoughts trouble your mind. I don't know about your past experiences or what you face right now. But God is saying to you: "You are a miracle in motion. I have already begun to work on your behalf. I am moving in your life. You must understand this."

When you repent, God is with you. Some things might look the way they've always looked, but God is with you. He didn't forsake you or leave you behind. He is fully invested in your story, and He won't write you off.

Say that to yourself: "God won't write me off!"

Instead, God will change the text of your life when you open the book of your heart. And opening that book means telling Him, "I am going to change, God. I know I need You more than anything else in my life."

Gideon was living in fear when God spoke to him. God said, "Things are not going well in your life right now, but right now you are mighty. This is how I see you."

Then God adds the word "valor," which means worth and significance. To have valor is to be valuable. God values you and me, just as He valued Gideon.

I don't know all of the facts about your life, but I do know the truth. And the truth will always change the facts of our lives.

Here's the truth:

> *"I know what I am planning for you," says the LORD. "I have good plans for you, not plans to hurt you. I will give you hope and a good future"* (Jeremiah 29:11 NCV).

With that truth in mind, let's close this chapter in prayer:

> Father, I thank You for every person reading this book. Every one of them is important and valuable to You. You pour out Your grace and mercy to all. Jesus died on the cross for all.
>
> You know everything ahead for each of us. In John's gospel, You remind us that Jesus came

into the world not to condemn it, but to save it. Thank You for sending Jesus to us.

May all of us see ourselves as Gideon came to see himself, as a person of strength and valor. We all have things we don't like about ourselves. We all get frustrated with the direction our stories seem to be headed. I ask You to calm the storms of our lives, to change our stories for the better, as we open our hearts to You, where the real change needs to begin.

Amen.

8

Everybody Is a Somebody!

By now, I hope you are growing familiar with one of this book's major themes: God can change the story of a city by changing the story of one person at a time. YOU are that person and this is your time! You are a somebody. In fact, everybody is a somebody!

Statements like the ones in the paragraph above raise an important question: Do you truly believe that every person is important in God's eyes? I hope you said "Yes!" Because they are! In God's eyes, everybody is a somebody, and every somebody has a story. Everybody's story, including yours, is important to God.

God is personally invested in our stories, as we saw with Gideon in the previous chapter. He wants us to live out our maximum spiritual potential. That's why I call Jesus the Story Changer. He can transform stories that seem hopeless. He can help us over insurmountable obstacles.

The story inside us changes, and when we change, the stories *around* us begin to change too. As we've been learning, all of our stories are connected.

God does not change stories through human strength, but through His supernatural strength. The apostle Paul reminds us, "[Not in your own strength] for it is God Who is all the while effectually at work in you [energizing and creating in you the power and desire], both to will and to work for His good pleasure *and* satisfaction *and* delight" (Philippians 2:13 AMPC). Indeed, when you have a personal encounter with Jesus, you have something supernatural going on in your life. It's miraculous!

God energizes you. He empowers you to do the good works that please Him and enrich the lives of those around you. This enriches your life as well. God gives us what some call The Mojo, The Holy Ghost Mojo, to be precise.

How does this work in real life? I want to show you by sharing the story of a couple from our church. They have offered to share their story to show how God's Spirit works, even in dire circumstances. Even when we feel broken—like nobodies instead of somebodies.

Marques and Nicole Farmer had been married for about nine years when this took place.

At the time, they had two young children, Moriah and Micaiah. They joined Word of Life in mid-2009. Before coming to

Word of Life, they had been very active in ministry at their previous churches, where they had been volunteering for six years nonstop. So when they came to Word of Life, they decided to take a break. "We were burned out," explains Marques. "We felt we deserved a little time off. That choice ended up costing us almost everything."

After awhile, Marques did start serving in a ministry called Life Connect. But Nicole had become so consumed with her job that she started to stray from the people who loved her most—her family and her friends.

Months passed and the couple found that they simply could not get along. "The tension in our home was unbearable due to the fighting and arguing" Marques admits. "We couldn't say anything to one another without one of us getting offended or hurt. Our arguments got worse. The verbal and physical abuse got worse. There was nothing we could do to control it."

As a result, the couple drifted further and further apart from each other, and from God.

"My marriage was rapidly fading away," Nicole says. "I became involved in an extra-marital affair."

After the affair began, Nicole confessed to her husband that she did not love him anymore, and that their marriage was not going to work.

"I wanted a divorce from my husband," Nicole admits.

"Nothing anybody could say or do would convince me otherwise."

Meanwhile, Marques felt guilty. "I knew that I had somehow allowed this to happen in my marriage and in my family," he explains. "I just didn't see a way out. I started coming to church more often because my heart longed for my relationship with God to be restored, and for my relationship with my wife to be restored."

For her part, Nicole knew she needed to get re-involved with ministry. "I felt like we pulled away from ministry and that was the reason our lives had been affected," she says. "We weren't serving in God's house, and we weren't serving God's people. We weren't under the covering that we were under before. Meanwhile, Marques was very adamant about not getting a divorce. I had no idea why. After all, he had just found out that I was cheating on him. It seemed like the common-sense thing to do. 'Why in the world do you want to stay with me?' I wondered.

Marques sought counseling with Pastor Chauncey, one of the assistant pastors at Word of Life. He asked Nicole to attend counseling with Pastor Donalee, who is Pastor Chauncey's wife. Nicole refused, initially.

"Finally, I agreed to sit down with her," Nicole recalls, "but I already *knew* I was doing something wrong. I didn't need somebody to sit there and tell me that."

At first, things did not improve for the Farmers. In fact, they got worse. "My wife left and didn't come home," Marques says. "I prayed daily for her, for the restoration of her relationship with God. After a while, she agreed to meet with Pastor Chauncey, Pastor Donalee, and me for marriage counseling."

Nicole explains, "When I sat down with Pastor Donalee, I opened up to her. I told her things I had never told anyone. She sat and listened with open ears. My husband and I met with the two pastors together, and they continually prayed for us and encouraged us and gave us things to work on at home. Even when I had no desire to work on my marriage, people continued to pray for me—the pastors and Vicky Chambliss, who was my Life Group Leader at the time. My husband bought me a jar that read 'Love Blooms Here.' Every morning, he put a mini love letter or an encouraging note or Scripture in the jar, which he set by the front door so that I would see it when I left the house.

"I said things like 'This is so stupid. I don't care about these letters. You're wasting your time.' Regardless of what I said, he wrote me a letter every single morning. Some days I wouldn't even read the letter, just out of spite. I moved out of our house. I left for my new place when the kids went to bed. Then I would come home early in the morning to get things situated. And every day when I came home, my husband would be on the couch praying for me."

Through the prayers and efforts of many people, the Holy Spirit began to speak to Nicole. "When we were getting ready for work one morning," she recalls, "my husband informed me that he had found a place to live and that he was going to go check it out after work that day. I told him immediately that I didn't want him to move out and that I wanted to work on restoring our marriage. From that day on, we prayed, and we made a commitment to God to work on our marriage, to let Him be the center of it and guide our steps."

Still, things didn't get better overnight. But they did get better day by day. Marques notes, "Pastor Chauncey and my life group leader, William Chambliss, were there for me. Will and his wife, Vicky, would come to our house. They live all the way on the other side of the island, but they took the time to visit us. They shared their testimony with us. Those people loved me and my wife through one of the most difficult times in our life. I can't even begin to explain to you what it meant to us to have them in our corner, to be supportive of us, to be understanding, and to be encouraging during our time of need."

Marques concludes, "We're a living witness that our church motto, 'Doing life together,' is not just a cliché. I don't know where I would have found the courage to move forward if not for the effort of the people here at Word of Life. They loved us back to life. We are forever grateful for the heart of this house, for the vision of this house, and for the standard that our pastor set for loving people back to life."

Isn't that an amazing true story of transformation! The Farmers endured a painful season in their marriage. Their story seemed hopeless. They felt like nobodies. Then Jesus showed up.

People from a church that loves Jesus showed up. This is an important part of this couple's story, because church should be a place of hope for people going through trouble and working on things in their lives.

As God worked through His people, this couple, this family, learned to seek God and to be in His presence. They discovered how to establish themselves in the Spirit so that they could see victory, even in the darkest of times. They learned to dwell not on the impossible, but on the *God* of the Impossible. To focus on the Circumstance Changer, rather than the mere circumstances themselves.

Marques and Nicole are living proof of how God changes the story of a city, one person at a time. God turned their time of testing into a testimony. Through that testimony, thousands of people are now hearing the Farmers' story and receiving its hope and encouragement: God will turn your trials into triumphs, your setbacks into comebacks.

Even when we are weak and broken, the joy of the Lord is our strength. (See Nehemiah 8:10.)

Through God's strength, you can see victory. You can have vision. Vision is the picture of your future, painted by faith, on the canvas of your imagination.

You are a somebody. I hope you have been encouraged by this story.

9

Conquering Your Worst Day

Satan is a master of intimidation. He's bent on keeping God's people locked in mindsets of fear, defeat, depression, anxiety, pain, discouragement, and disappointment. The devil attempts to make life seem impossible, unchangeable, unalterable, and unresolvable. But his plans are not the final word! God always has the final word! This is why Psalms 43:19 (NKJV) states, "Many are the afflictions of the righteous, but the Lord delivers him out of them all."

In life, things happen: unexpected, unwanted, undesired and undeserved things. We all have good days and bad days, and all of our stories will contain adversity. But what do you do on the worst day of your life? Throw in the towel? Quit?

Give up? No! Faith is the key substance needed for what to do on the worst day of your life. What is faith? It is trusting God in the midst of whatever you are going through.

WHAT IS FAITH? IT IS TRUSTING GOD IN THE MIDST OF WHATEVER YOU ARE GOING THROUGH.

Please keep that last sentence in mind as we explore this chapter. The outcome of our stories will hinge on how well we use our faith in God.

There was a man who learned to overcome the worst day of his life. His name is David. As a young man, he was anointed as Israel's future king. God was working in his life, especially during his worst days, but David didn't always realize this. We also have trouble seeing God's hand at work in our lives when we face setbacks. "If God is working in my life," we wonder, "why is everything going wrong?"

Well, for every setback God has a comeback. And every comeback is a triumph of His grace. Our flops and failures do not disqualify us from being used by God. They don't disqualify us from receiving God's best in our lives.

I need to say it again: God has a comeback for your every setback.

He is never done with a person as long as he or she will keep an open heart. God doesn't offer a "problem-free pass" to success. We have to walk it out by faith. David had to walk his faith out in order to face his setbacks. Some were minor, but some were major. He faced many enemies, the greatest of which was David himself. David is living proof of the verse, "Many are the afflictions of the righteous, but the LORD delivers him out of them all" (Psalms 34:19 NKJV).

The book of 1 Samuel, chapter 30, reveals a portion of David's turbulent life. I hope a glimpse of his story will help you understand how God is working in your life right now, even in the midst of hardship.

GOD HAS A COMEBACK FOR YOUR EVERY SETBACK.

Some context is important here. The year was 1012, B.C. David was 29 years old. He had lived a life of adventure. As a teenage boy, the prophet Samuel came to his home in Bethlehem and anointed him as the future King of Israel. A few months later, young David was thrust into sudden fame when he killed Goliath, the champion of the Philistines. After that, David moved on from caring for his father's sheep and became a member of the royal household of King Saul. King Saul made David the commander of his armies. David led the armies of Israel in one victory after another. As a daring young warrior, David became the national hero. King Saul killed his thousands, but David killed his tens of thousands. King Saul became so jealous that he tried to kill David, and David had to flee.

The "future king" became a fugitive. He went from being a

national hero to an outcast on the run. For several years, David and the 600 men who chose to follow him roamed the hillside of Judea. He continued to fight the Philistines and expanded and secured the borders of Israel. Meanwhile, David waited for the fulfillment of Samuel's prophecy that he would be the next king of Israel.

He guided his group of men to a place called Ziklag, where they made a temporary home for all of their families for the next year and a half. Ziklag was an "in-between" place for David. It wasn't Bethlehem, the place where he started and it wasn't Jerusalem, the place of his destiny. We all spend some time in Ziklag, the place "in-between" where we started and where we are headed, the place of patient waiting. It is not where we came from or where we're going. It is just where we happen to be for a season.

It was in Ziklag that David would experience one of the worst days of his life. It's vital we understand the gravity of the situation here. David probably started off having a normal day. He's leading his 600 mighty men back to their home in Ziklag after taking a three-day journey, and he sees columns of smoke rising up in the distance from Ziklag. The men grow silent. Then it's pandemonium. They rush to Ziklag, terrified over the fate of their families and friends. They were horrified by what they saw. It had been attacked, ransacked, and set on fire by the Amalekites. They had stolen everything. Every home had been reduced to a smoldering heap of rubble. They torched the city and kidnapped all the inhabitants of the city. This was David's worst day.

Imagine arriving at your hometown and finding everything burnt to the ground. Nothing remains but smoking ruins.

You would be at a breaking point. A breaking point is a life event that will either break you down or inspire you to break through. It's a defining moment. The enemy wants you to give up. The Holy Spirit wants you to overcome. God's Spirit encourages you, "Know that this is not the time to break down. God is not done with your story. He is with you still. This tragedy does not mean that God has given up on you. In fact, He has wonderful things He wants to do in your life."

When something goes wrong in your life, please remember that you are not defeated or forgotten. David's story did not end at Ziklag. Your story does not have to end at a negative place either.

As you think about your story, what is your own personal Ziklag, your "in-between?" Is it a low point in a friendship? Is it a career setback? Is it a challenge with a son or daughter? Is it a bad report from the doctor?

> **THIS TRAGEDY DOES NOT MEAN THAT GOD HAS GIVEN UP ON YOU. IN FACT, HE HAS WONDERFUL THINGS HE WANTS TO DO IN YOUR LIFE.**

This "somewhere in-between" does not always feel good. But God is true to His Word. He's going to watch over His promises to you.

Let's remember that David was just a young man of faith when he faced Ziklag. He had no idea how his life would turn out.

And what is faith? It's trusting God in the midst of your "in-between," even though circumstances are grim. David lost everything, and now his 600 men wanted to kill him. But David kept trusting God and His promises. We should do the same. God is not done with us. He will get us through our "in-betweens." When you get discouraged, keep reminding yourself, "My story is not done yet. I'm just somewhere in-between."

Between prophecy and destiny stands a Ziklag, a time of testing. When we choose, as David did, to walk by faith, our Ziklag becomes the crucible in which our faith is forged. It is where we learn to face life as a conqueror– no, more than a conqueror! After a time of grieving, David pursued the Amalekites and routed them in a grueling 24-hour battle. He and his men recovered everything that the enemy had carried away—people and property.

So I ask you again: What is your Ziklag? Perhaps you are several years into your marriage, and things are not going the way you want them to. You had this idea that your marriage was going to be glorious. Blessings from heaven would fall on the two of you every day. It would be like a modern Garden of Eden. Nobody or nothing could wipe the smiles off the faces of you and your spouse.

Then what happened? Trouble. It can happen five years or five minutes into a marriage. You can start to doubt. "Is this marriage God's will?" you wonder. Relax. It's not that you are suddenly out of God's will; it's just that you are somewhere "in-between." You might think that your spouse needs to change or your marriage is in big trouble.

Perhaps it's you who needs to change.

I'd like to speak to the husbands right now. In love, and with all due respect, I urge you to man up. Realize that God has a great plan for your life story, and that includes your marriage.

I also want you to realize that God is not mad at you. He's trying to help you. This is an opportunity for you to change for the better. Today's church needs husbands who will be of good courage. Don't walk out on church. Don't walk out on your wives. Don't walk out on your children. Stand your ground.

Don't play those macho games, which are so easy to fall into. Don't try to intimidate your family. The truly manly thing to do is to love somebody, care for somebody. Embrace your children. Build up your wife. Your leadership position in the family comes from God. He knows you are the head of the household. You don't need to go around proving that fact to your wife and children. Instead, I encourage you to live out your leadership.

Wives, I encourage you to be a partner to your husbands. Work together, and respect each other's strengths. Help set a positive tone for your household. Appreciate all that your husband does—and you will find that you are appreciated too.

Now, let's get back to David. The city of Ziklag was not his only "Ziklag." He would go on to lose his best friend, Jonathan, in battle. He would commit adultery and have a man murdered. He would have an especially difficult relationship with one of his sons. But he kept on allowing God to rewrite the text of his life, by keeping the book of his heart open.

This is what I will keep urging you to do throughout this book. Remember that God is changing your story. You might be experiencing a life crisis right now. But God has not stopped writing.

You didn't get the new job you applied for? God has not stopped writing.

A close friend betrayed you? God has not stopped writing.

You got cut from the team? God has not stopped writing.

You committed a major sin? God has not stopped writing.

Keep the book of your heart open. Don't close the book.

With these thoughts in mind, let's look at how David escaped from his "Ziklag."

First, he wept. He showed emotion. He understood that just because you have faith in God, that does not mean you won't experience negative feelings. As David wrote in Psalms 62:8, "Trust in him at all times, you people; pour out your hearts to him, for God is our refuge" (NIV).

Second, David refused to become bitter. He refused to blame God or anyone else for his troubles. So many people play the blame game when they get bitter. But bitterness never solves a problem. Bitterness only makes a bad situation worse.

Third, he encouraged himself in God. As 1 Samuel 30:6 explains, "David was greatly distressed because the men were talking of stoning him; each one was bitter in spirit. . . . But David found strength in the LORD his God" (NIV). Let's focus on the significance

WHEN WE TURN TO GOD WE WILL BEGIN TO GET OUR JOY BACK.

of this verse. David's own men were ready to revolt against him because of what had happened to their families.

But David understood something vital: When there is no one else to turn to, you can turn to God. Praise Him. Change your focus. Say to yourself, "My God is bigger than this problem!" When we turn to God we will begin to get our joy back.

As David wrote in another Psalm . . .

*"I'm sure now I'll see God's goodness in the exu-
berant earth. Stay with GOD! Take heart. Don't
quit. I'll say it again: Stay with GOD"* (Psalms
27:13-14 MSG).

Fourth, David got mad at the devil. Not at God, not at
the men he was leading, but at the actual source of misery.
He decided to break the devil's hold on his life so that he could
move on in his story.

It's important to follow David's example here and not allow
the devil a foothold. Remember one of this book's key themes:
What you tolerate—including the devil's schemes and lies—you
authorize to stay in your life!

Now let's look at two more stories, from the New Testament.
In Mark Chapter 5, Jesus is approached by a madman living
in a cemetery. "He lived there among the tombs and graves.
No one could restrain him—he couldn't be chained, couldn't
be tied down. He had been tied many times with chains and
ropes, but he broke the chains, snapped the ropes. . . . Night
and day he roamed through the graves and hills, screaming out
and slashing himself with sharp stones. When he saw Jesus . . .
he ran and bowed in worship before him—then bellowed in
protest, 'What business do you have, Jesus, Son of the High

God, messing with me? I swear to God, don't give me a hard time!' (Jesus had just commanded the tormenting evil spirit, 'Out! Get out of the man!')

"Jesus asked him, 'Tell me your name.'

"He replied, 'My name is Mob. I'm a rioting mob.' Then he desperately begged Jesus not to banish him from the country. A large herd of pigs was browsing and rooting on a nearby hill. The demons begged him, 'Send us to the pigs so we can live in them.'

"Jesus gave the order. . . . Crazed, they [the pigs] stampeded over a cliff into the sea and drowned" (Mark 5:1-13 MSG).

The next time we meet the "madman," he is wearing decent clothes and speaking rationally and calmly. The man asks to accompany Jesus on his travels, but Jesus says no. He tells the man, "Go home to your own people. Tell them your story—what the Master did, how he had mercy on you" (verses 18-19).

The man obeys. He begins to preach in the Ten Towns area, proclaiming what Jesus has done for him. He becomes the talk of the town, no . . . towns.

Talk about someone once stuck in his story! This guy was literally a dead man walking. No one could help him. No one could even control him. Then Jesus showed up. Note that Jesus never asked the man, "How did you get like this? Why are you roaming around the tombs?"

So many people live in "tombs" today. Tombs called Addiction, Pain, Hopelessness, and Guilt. They think they have been forgotten, just like the so-called Madman of Gadara (or Gerasenes). I am here to assure you that you are not forgotten. You are not insignificant. When God sees you, He sees a Somebody. A Somebody with a future and a hope.

Shortly after healing the demon-possessed man from the tombs, Jesus encounters a blind beggar named Bartimaeus. When he hears that Jesus is near, Bartimaeus cries out, "Son of David, Jesus! Mercy, have mercy on me!" (Mark 10:48 MSG).

Some people try to silence Bartimaeus, but that just makes him turn up the volume. Jesus calls the man over. Bartimaeus throws off his coat (symbolizing his desire to leave his past behind him) and approaches Jesus. Jesus asks, "What can I do for you?"

Bartimaeus's answer is simple: "Rabbi, I want to see" (Mark 10:51).

"On your way," Jesus assures him. "Your faith has saved and healed you" (Mark 10:52).

Instantly, the man receives his sight. He follows Jesus down the road.

This story comprises only a few verses, but it is rich in meaning. First, the story takes place in Jericho, one of the oldest and lowest cities of the time. It was home to the begging and the broke, the busted and disgusted. The message for us is clear: Jesus will come to our "Jericho." He will meet us in the lowlands of our life.

Second, Bartimaeus is the son of Timaeus, a name that means "unclean" or "leper." The name Bartimaeus, then, was a label. But Jesus gave him a new identity.

Despite all that he had going against him, Bartimaeus was a good theologian. He knew Jesus had fed multitudes and raised the dead, so he reasoned, "If Jesus worked miracles in Jerusalem and Bethesda, why not here in Jericho? If Jesus has healed, delivered, blessed, and changed others . . . why not me?"

Here are four lessons we can learn from this blind beggar:

1. Bartimaeus was not content to be a spectator. He didn't want to watch Jesus; he wanted to *experience* Him. Likewise, we should seek a personal relationship with Jesus. He shouldn't be compartmentalized to Sunday mornings. Prayer, meditation, Scripture reading, and worship are all ways to experience our Lord.

2. He was not content with being quiet. He was brave and vulnerable enough to give voice to the cry of his heart. We should do the same. We should be honest and open before Jesus.

3. He was determined to get Jesus' attention. He would not be silenced by the people around him. He ignored those who said, "If it was God's will for you to see, you would have been healed by now. Give it up!" And once he had Jesus' attention, he was willing to ask for help. We should all seek this kind of persistence and determination.

4. He gave voice to his faith. He gave a faith-shout. He believed Jesus could restore his sight, and he said so. It's good to be bold. Jesus loves it when we proclaim our faith in confidence. When we say what we believe, no matter who is around to hear.

In short, Bartimaeus had an expectation that produced a *manifestation*.

He reached out in faith to the Savior who restores lost causes, mends broken hearts, and rescues the lost. The Jesus who gives hope to the hopeless.

This book is a book of hope. This time of your life, no matter what the circumstances, is a time of hope. This is the time to determine that you are going to keep the book open. Do not close the book on your marriage, your children, or your career. Don't close the book on your relationship with God.

I realize that some of you reading this might be divorced or abandoned in some way by a friend or business associate. Some of you are struggling with the multiple demands of being a single parent. Please don't close the book. You are not at the end of a sad story. You are just somewhere in-between, like David, Bartimaeus, and the demon-possessed man from Gerasenes.

Please say it out loud: "I will not close the book."

Because God will not close the book on you. He will not write you off. He is full of mercy. Rescue is right around the corner.

10

Silencing Your Loudest Critic

Even a positive guy like me has to admit it:

The world is full of critics.

We must guard ourselves against these critics, or they will ruin our stories.

One of our most loud and dangerous critics is the spirit of negativity. We have all experienced being hit with negative comments that stole our confidence and damaged our self -worth. None of us wants someone raining negativity on us, do we?

Please realize that when you are born again, the spirit of negativity, that's so prevalent in the world, no longer has to control you. The Bible promises us that we are delivered, set free.

Unfortunately, we sometimes like to cling to a few relics of our past, like negativity. Some people let negativity invade their stories because they don't realize they are no longer required to tolerate it. Others seem to like being cynical, looking down on others, "raining on everyone's parade." I am here to warn you that negativity is a formidable enemy of life. It hinders ordinary people from becoming extraordinary. It keeps us from experiencing the changes we yearn for in life.

Negativity is a blessing blocker. Often, there are subtle ways that we get talked into accepting negative mindsets and negative speech.

Fortunately, we have weapons to silence negativity. First, we must understand that we've been given the power of choice. If we make the right choices, we don't have to keep running into brick walls. We don't have to live a defeated life. Yes, challenges pop up, but we can navigate around them, as the Holy Spirit leads and guides us.

Second, we must realize how our beliefs about ourselves profoundly influence our lives. That's why it is so important to understand our identity in Christ.

At the same time, we need to be aware when incorrect beliefs about ourselves are affecting our lives. For example, a man who believes he is unemployable might not even try to create a resume or go interview for jobs. If we think we are unworthy of success, we won't strive for it. We won't try to climb that mountain, pursue that dream.

In other words, if you think you're an unwise person, you

might make unwise choices. But is that the choice any of us truly wants to make? The Bible cuts to the chase: "Choose life, so that you and your children will live" (Deuteronomy 30:19 MSG).

In life, the enemy called negativity can sneak up on us and cause us to make bad choices. We can subtly get lured into a negative mind-set. I want to give you four reasons why negativity is so dangerous, even crippling, as we try to make our life stories the best they can be. And I want to offer solutions as well.

First, negativity is a sign of inner defeat. Specifically, negativity affects the way we think, the way we view life, and the way we talk about life with others. Think about how these factors influence the story of you. The way we think, perceive, and speak can lead to success or failure in life.

Let's start with speech. Jesus said, "For the mouth speaks what the heart is full of" (Matthew 12:34 NIV). Have you ever confronted a person for speaking negatively?

What was the response? Was it, "I'm not being negative; I'm just keepin' it real. I am merely being realistic."

Did you tell the person, "It's possible to be realistic without being so negative"?

What about you? Do you reflect on what you say and how you say it? It's important to do this, because the words you speak spring from how you view the world . . . and yourself. I need to be blunt here: When we speak negatively, we are verbalizing inner defeat. We are verbalizing the direct opposite of faith in God! Negative speech limits our lives like almost nothing else. It robs us of hope.

Tragically, most people are unaware of negativity's impact on daily life—how it robs us of our God-given destiny.

NEGATIVE SPEECH LIMITS OUR LIVES LIKE ALMOST NOTHING ELSE. IT ROBS US OF HOPE.

A negative person is afraid to hope in anything, because he or she believes that hope will be crushed. There is this viewpoint of, "If I never hope, I'll never have to be disappointed" or "If I never trust anyone, I'll never have to face betrayal." The list can go on and on. This is not the way God wants us to think.

I find it interesting that many of us blame other people for the negativity in our lives. We blame our boss, our spouse, our friends, even our neighborhood or city.

Others blame circumstances. Have you heard someone say, "I've been so wronged in my life. No one has ever truly cared about me"? However, the Bible says that we all face trials and tribulation. We all pass through the Valley of Baca (an Old Testament valley also known as The Valley of Weeping). This valley was barren and devoid of water.

But the Bible also says that those who pass through the Valley of Weeping shall be blessed. (See Psalms 84:6.)

God doesn't command us, "Stay in the valley." Instead, He urges, "Get through that valley, by My power." He wants us to mind our viewpoints and our thinking when we encounter life's valleys.

We should all take care as we speak and think about our futures. Our speech and thoughts can become self-fulfilling prophecies. Have you heard someone say, "I told you I wouldn't get that promotion" or "I told you I wouldn't earn that scholarship"?

I want to lovingly remind these folks, "You're trying to determine the outcome before it has even come to pass. If you stop talking all that negativity over yourself, you will enjoy better results."

I understand that everyone faces challenges. They are unavoidable. But you can determine your perspective. You have control over your thought life and your words. How we understand, think, and speak about our lives *matters*.

Second, negativity never, ever examines itself. The most negative people I know are also the least self-aware people. Think about that for a moment. Isn't this true in your life as well?

And why are these negative folks so un-self-aware? They are too busy examining other people to take a good honest look at themselves.

The Bible advises us, "Examine yourselves to see if your faith is genuine. Test yourselves" (2 Corinthians 13:5 NLT).

Do you know Christians who disagree with a pastor or other church leader? They say things like, "I don't believe that faith stuff works the way my pastor says it does."

Who are these people actually disagreeing with? Jesus said we should walk by faith and not by sight. (See 2 Corinthians 5:7.) Jesus said that the just shall live by faith. People think they are arguing with a mere man when they are arguing with God.

I have heard people say, "I don't believe in the power of prayer." Really? Because God's Word says, "Instead of worrying, pray. Let petitions and praises shape your worries into prayers, letting God know your concerns. Before you know it, a sense of God's wholeness, everything coming together for good, will come and settle you down. It's wonderful what happens when Christ displaces worry at the center of your life" (Philippians 4:6 MSG).

What an amazing Scripture for all of us to remember!

I have also heard, "I don't believe in the power of 'speaking to' things. That verse about 'speak unto the mountain?' I mean, really, who is going to speak to a mountain?"

All I can say in response is this: "Jesus said to speak to that mountain, so you better speak to it." (See Mark 11:23.)

Of course, Jesus was using the mountain as a symbol of our

problems. We should speak to those problems. Jesus wants us to live the Kingdom way, not the world's way. Romans 12:2 reminds us, "Do not conform to the pattern of this world, but be transformed by the renewing of your mind" (NIV).

If we truly want to change our stories, if we truly want to see God's best, we must think and live His way. We must be self-aware, self-examining people.

Third, negativity always chooses the wrong friends.

The old adage "Opposites attract" does not apply to negativity. Have you noticed that negative people seem to attract other negative people—rather than positive people? You can put a million people in a huge stadium, and the only two negative people in the place will find each other. It's like they have radar. One negative person will say to the other, "You're the only one here who 'gets me.'"

Negativity is foolish. It creates a mind-set and a way of speaking that are contrary to God's Word. And when you get two or more foolish people together, watch out!

I encourage you—be very careful how you allow people to speak things into your life. Are people moving you toward your destiny? Are they encouraging you to fulfill your life's purpose? Do they encourage you in your walk with God? Do they comfort you when you're down? Do they strengthen you, or do they drain the life right out of you?

Fourth, negativity will keep you from being productive. We all want to live productive lives. We want the best for ourselves and our families. Philemon 1:6 says, "I pray that your partnership with us in the faith may be effective in deepening your understanding of every good thing we share for the sake of Christ" (NIV).

I want to focus on the phrase "every good thing we share for the sake of Christ." We have good things in us, no matter what is going on around us. Our faith becomes *effective* when we acknowledge these good things.

The moment you are born again, your heart is changed. A deposit is made in your heart, making it the treasure of your life. Upon that deposit, you can build your life. Your life is not built on the outside things all around you. Your strength is inside. It's not about accumulating the stuff outside.

That faith inside you works *for* you. Faith moves mountains, including the mountain called Negativity. Faith pleases God. Faith changes your story. Faith helps you change other people's stories.

Our verse in Philemon says that the release (or communication) of our faith is effective—or "effectual," in some translations. The release of our faith becomes productive when we acknowledge every good thing inside us. To acknowledge means to recognize the truth of something. And the truth is that you have been born again, regardless of what chaos might be swirling around you. It doesn't matter what the economy is doing or what that negative boss, relative, or friend is always telling you. There is something great inside you!

We must be on our guard, because the spirit of negativity will try to contaminate that inner greatness. This spirit wants you to obsess about past mistakes and past failures. This spirit wants to hold you back. To get you stuck on a negative page of your story and never move forward.

But what about all the good things in life? Why do so many of us fret over long lists of the bad in our lives, but we never remind ourselves of all the good stuff? All the successes. All the answered prayers. All the blessings. All of the kind words people have spoken to or written about us.

I encourage you to look at yourself in the mirror and say, "You know what? There is something good inside me. I don't care what happened in my past. There is something good inside of me right now!"

That's the truth about you. God wants us to acknowledge every good thing He placed in us (Philemon 1:6). Not the truth according to Art Sepulveda or Word of Life. According to God Himself.

As we wrap up this chapter, remember that negativity is a disease. It's a disease that tries to limit your story and contaminate the treasure in your heart. The Bible assures you of the good things inside of you. God knows every path you have walked in your story. He knows where you have failed and fallen. Yet He loves you and believes in you—more than you believe in yourself. God is the one who put the hope inside you. He deems you worthy of that hope. You and I are indeed worthy of every good thing in us in Christ Jesus.

God didn't make a mistake when He made you. His perfect will for you is to acknowledge your every good thing. *Believe* what He says. Not kinda-sorta, believe. Not believe on Sundays only. Believe every day of every week of every year!

When you're on the job, there is good inside you. When you're home with your family, there is good inside you. Even when things go wrong—someone just rear-ended you at the stop light. There is still something good inside you. When you get that unexpected monster of a bill from the doctor? There is something good inside you.

I urge you to start living from the inside out. Remember, the Bible calls it being transformed by the renewing of your mind (See Romans 12:2.) Start living out of the treasure you have on the inside. And I'm not talking about those "treasures in heaven" here. Remember 2 Corinthians 4:7: "But we have this treasure in jars of clay to show that this all-surpassing power is from God and not from us" (NIV).

These jars of clay represent our earthen vessels, our flesh suits. There is a treasure of power, right now, inside you. That is different from the treasures to come in heaven.

Think of God's power in you as your potential. This is your inheritance. You have a right to use it. The outcome of your story hinges on whether or not you will unleash your faith, your God Potential.

Paul urged Timothy to "fan into flame the gift of God. . . ." (2 Timothy 1:6 NIV).

This is my encouragement to you as well. Please realize you're more powerful than others have ever given you credit for. Stop listening to the devil's lies. Don't accept any negativity. Anything that speaks opposite of what God says about you is a lie from hell. God wants you to value the good things inside you. Tap into your inner, Christ-fueled power.

Imagine with me what God can do in your life. He has no limits. He is ready to change our stories. We are the ones who hesitate, doubt, and allow the spirit of negativity to drag us down. Don't let anyone or anything make you believe change is impossible. Nothing is impossible with God. When He finds someone willing to live by faith in Him, He can make a story amazing.

He can make *your* story amazing. I'm positive.

As the Father has sent Me, I also send you.

—JESUS

11

Faith: The Controlling Factor

As I have been praying about this book, a verse has lingered in my mind: "But seek first the kingdom of God and His righteousness, and all these things shall be added to you" (Matthew 6:33 NKJV).

With promises like this, why do believers still fail to walk in the fullness of the Christian life? I wonder about this a lot, because there have been times in my life when I've needed to take a long, honest look at how I was living out my faith. We must all ask ourselves the question, "Is my faith in God's Word the controlling factor in my life?" In other words, what influences my decisions more: God's Word or my emotions?

Day by day, we should become steadier in our walk of faith, so that our faith in God influences us more than our own emotions.

This is what I mean by faith being the controlling factor in our lives. With this in mind, let's take another look at the Scripture that began this chapter. "But first and most importantly seek (aim at, strive after) His kingdom and His righteousness. . . ." (Amplified Bible). This translation goes on to explain that righteousness is "His way of doing and being right."

There is, indeed, a way to do life right. Conversely, there are ways that only *seem* right. But they are not. In my life, the adversary has tried to entice me to follow certain paths, such as the Path of My Limited Perspective or The Path of My Own Logic. Because I am a Christian and a pastor, those paths can appear right to me. But they are not right. I love what Solomon says in Proverbs 14:12: "There is a way that seems right to a man, But its end is the way of death" (NKJV). Death, in this verse, includes defeat or failure, not necessarily one's ultimate demise.

Like you, I want to live a meaningful and effective life, to be productive in my professional and personal lives. But there is humanity's way to do this, and then there is God's way.

In Matthew 6, Jesus is speaking to His disciples, and to all who have hearts to listen to Him. He encourages them to live God's way, first and foremost. How do we do that? How do we handle our relationships the right way? How do we face the many situations that confront us day after day?

These are vital questions because there are a lot of people who say they love God, but they really have no respect for Him. And some of those people can be found in church every Sunday.

When someone does not respect God, he does not have a reverence for God. He doesn't view God with awe and wonder. And if you lack this respect, you will have a hard time doing what God says to do. God's Word is just another option for you, depending on how you feel on a given day. There is no commitment to follow God's Word, to live it out, regardless of circumstance or emotion.

Sometimes, people wonder, "Why am I not seeing better results in my life? I am a Christian. I attend church. Maybe I should start following my own logic."

If you have thoughts like this, please remember that we have an adversary. He wants to trick all of us. Titles do not matter to him. He wants to trick me, a pastor, and he wants to trick you, whatever your title or occupation. Our adversary is no respecter of titles.

But Jesus assures us, "Anyone who loves me will obey my teaching. My Father will love them, and we will come to them and make our home with them" (John 14:23 NIV).

Note the first part of verse 23: "Anyone who loves me. . . ." This is our guidepost. If I claim to love God, then I must obey

His Word. On the other hand, as Jesus says in the very next verse, "Anyone who does not love me will not obey my teaching" (John 14:24 NIV).

This Scripture really clears things up for us. The Christian life is not about emotions or circumstances. We have specific instructions on how to live the abundant life. However, we need to keep our minds or our emotions from taking over.

Have you ever felt emotionally justified when you said or did something? You felt something powerful and you let it out. I have to raise my hand on that one. Something can feel so right, but, based on the Bible, it is so wrong. Maybe you're raising your hand right now too.

Have you ever said, or heard someone say, "I feel like this new job is the right one for me" or "I feel like I should start a relationship with this person I met online"?

And away we go . . . "I feel, I feel, I feel."

Yes, feelings are important. God gave them to us for a reason. They are part of our humanity, and we cannot deny them. They are a part of life. And emotion is part of love. But our love for God must transcend emotion.

Here's what that means in practical terms. Some people will stop going to church because they don't feel like it anymore. Or they skip from one church to another because of how a church makes them feel. Some people even blame these feelings on the

Holy Spirit. "I just feel like the Holy Spirit was leading me to leave my church and find a new one!" they might say.

I call these folks Charismatic Cruisers. They blame the Holy Spirit for their decisions, when, in fact, those decisions are made purely on emotion. You can't get far in your spiritual walk this way. Over the course of time, I see people who have only inched forward, if they have made any progress at all. They lack the sense of direction and the resolve to make the correct decisions.

I guarantee you that God wants better results for you. After all, you are the living example of Him on Earth. Amen? Tell yourself, "God wants me to prosper."

Sadly, when the Charismatic Cruisers fail to prosper, they blame God. They say, "I guess those Bible promises do not apply to modern life."

I am here to tell you that the promises do apply. In fact, God is obligated to fulfill His promises. He keeps His word. He confirms what the Bible says. God performs more than lip service. He expects the same of us.

God wants you to break through, not break down. His Word will uphold you and me if only we will do things God's way. This will not always be comfortable. Sometimes, it will be an emotional struggle. For example, have you ever tried to forgive someone you simply do not feel like forgiving? Have you tried to speak kindly and lovingly to someone who is responding with hateful talk or sarcasm? You'd like to give 'em a piece of your mind, not the peace of Christ. Believe me, I understand. It is very hard to speak words of grace when we'd like to speak words of wrath. It takes overcoming the power of our emotions.

Here is some practical advice: The situations I describe in the paragraph above are defining moments in life. Christianity is not complicated. Jesus urges, "Just follow My Word and you're going to come out on top. I will prosper you."

GOD WANTS YOU TO BREAK THROUGH, NOT BREAK DOWN.

But many Christians cannot follow this leading—or at least not follow it consistently. Then they shake their heads and wonder why God is not blessing them. Please understand: God will never stop loving us. But unconditional love does not mean you will live a blessed life story.

This is a vital truth, so let me elaborate: We cannot substitute God's love for living a blessed life. I know many Christians who are loved by God, but they struggle in their stories. They cannot break through financially. They cannot free themselves from negative emotions that have them all tangled up.

I am reminded of something my pastor, Cesar Castellanos, told me: "If I change, everything changes." I am here to tell you that if we will devote ourselves to God's Word, His blessings will go into motion.

Understand, however, that doing things God's way means giving up some things, cutting off some things.

Jesus put this in graphic terms. He said that if your eye causes you to stumble, you should pluck it out. If your hand gets you into trouble, cut it off. (See Matthew 5:29-30.) Fortunately, He was not being literal! But He was being blunt about our being committed enough to get rid of whatever holds us back.

First John 2:5 reminds us, "But whoever keeps His word, truly the love of God is perfected in him. By this we know that we are in Him" (NKJV). On the other hand, failing to keep God's Word will only frustrate us.

Trust me on this. So many times in my personal story I have needed to love people beyond my emotional capacity, and my emotional want-to. Further, I have needed to love beyond what made sense intellectually. I tell you in all honesty, if it were not for God's Word, I would not have been able to do this. I don't think I am any different from most people in this regard.

We all have to choose how we are going to live on this planet. You can choose to be a church-goer and still not be a very good Christian. Many people go to church. Then they walk out the doors to be as angry, bitter, unforgiving, and emotionally abusive as anyone.

Don't get me wrong; I'm glad they keep going to church, because that way the Word of God has a chance to change them.

They can make a change, and the Holy Spirit will be there to confirm that change in their lives.

My spiritual journey began well before I was a pastor. Yes, there are things you do not do once you are a pastor, but there are more things you *do* simply because you are a Christian. I am a Christian before I am a pastor. My standard is not my title. My standard is not based on accomplishments. My standard for life is found in God's Word.

Before I realized this truth, it was all about my emotions. It was all about how I sized up my problems. It was all about what I could figure out. It was all about what I could manipulate, maneuver, or trick my way into getting—socially, financially, and so on. This was how I led my life in general. That gets tiring after a while. It really wore me down.

So, please believe me: If you want to live a full and enjoyable life—if you want to have truly meaningful relationships and a meaningful career—the Bible promises that God's hand of favor is upon your life, upon your personal story!

WE LIKE TO BELIEVE OUR EMOTIONS, BUT OUR EMOTIONS DON'T ALWAYS TELL US THE TRUTH.

As we bring this chapter to a close, I must repeat: There is our way of doing and being right, and there is God's way. Jesus faced this truth in His own life. He faced those breaking points that become defining moments.

He showed us that if our standard is not the Word, we can be misled by emotions. He told His Father, "[N]ot my will, but yours be done" (Luke 22:42 NIV) even though He was in agony. We like to believe our emotions, but our emotions don't always tell us the truth. The truth, not our emotions, sets us free!

So many people are not free emotionally. They are governed by anxieties and fears. They are cowered by intimidation. When you are intimidated, you act out of fear. Too many of us live by emotion, because we have no other standard. Have you heard someone say, "Hey, this is my reality. This is how I feel about it"?

I sympathize with such people. I feel a lot of things too. I feel them deeply. I have strong emotions when it comes to my marriage and my relationship with my children. I feel a lot of things as my friendships evolve. But here is

> **I DO NOT HAVE TO ACT ON EVERYTHING I FEEL. EMOTIONS ARE A WARNING SYSTEM, NOT A CALL TO ACTION!**

what I am learning: I do not have to act on everything I feel. Emotions are not a call to action. They should be more like a warning system. A warning system, but not a guidepost!

We all face breaking points in life. The Bible is full of men and women who faced defining moments and had to either break down or break through.

By God's grace and power, they broke through. That is my prayer for you and the story of your life.

Say to yourself, "I'm not breaking down! I'm breaking through!"

I know that you will.

12

From Breaking Point
to Breakthrough

I n the previous chapter, I referred to one of Jesus' defining moments. Now I would like to reveal more of that story.

In Matthew chapter 26, verses 36-46, we find Jesus going to pray in the Garden of Gethsemane. It's important to understand that Gethsemane is a Hebrew term meaning "olive press." Here was a place where olives were gathered into sacks and stacked one upon another. A beam was lowered on the stack. Increasing amounts of weight were added to the beam, so that the oil would be pressed from the olives.

Isn't it interesting that Jesus chose Gethsemane? He could have gone anywhere to pray. Why an olive press and not a mountain top or sea side? Because He is going to show us what to do under the pressures of life.

He has his 12 disciples along. He asks three of them (Peter, James, and John) to follow Him. In Matthew 26:38, Jesus says, "Stay here and keep watch with me." In verse 41, when Jesus returned to his disciples and found them sleeping, He told them, "Watch and pray..." (NIV).

Jesus is ready to give them an illustration. He's going to be the living example. He doesn't need to draw anything on a chalkboard. He Himself is going to be the life example.

Here's how He does it. Jesus did not go to Gethsemane by accident. He knew what was about to happen to Him. He was going to die on the cross for all of humanity. He came to Earth to seek and save the lost.

He had followed God's direction for His life, and now He was at a breaking point, where He would either break down or break through. God wants to show you how to break through. Jesus is the perfect example.

In this garden, Jesus becomes sorrowful and deeply distressed. He tells Peter, James, and John, "This sorrow is crushing my life out" (Matthew 26:36 MSG).

Verses like this should remind us that Jesus understands our emotions. He was sorrowful and deeply distressed. There's nothing wrong with having emotions. Jesus Himself had emotions. Emotions are part of our life stories. Wouldn't our stories be rather dull if they lacked feeling? We are not bad Christians because we have strong feelings. We just cannot let our emotions control us above and beyond what God's Word says.

What Christians need to do is take control of our emotions. We need to manage our anger, for example, rather than allowing that anger to manage us. This requires God's Word and the work of the Holy Spirit. As noted in the previous chapter, emotions are like the warning system of the human body—physically speaking. We need them, but we need to learn how to control our emotions, lest they, without restraint, begin to control our lives.

Meanwhile, if you know anything about the Gethsemane story, you know what happens next. Jesus has shared with three disciples that His soul is sorrowful "even unto death." What do they do? They fall asleep—and they do it three times!

This is an odd time for disciples to nap on the job. But this is not just about physical tiredness. It is a subtle attack spiritually. So many people fall asleep when it comes to prayer. They lose their sense of alertness when life pressures become overwhelming. Prayer, on the other hand, opens the door for God to move on our behalf.

Jesus is deeply grieved. The King James translation says He felt "very heavy." Have you ever felt very heavy? Like there was so much pressure on your life? I have felt that way many times—burdened in my mind, worn out in my body, and feeling empty spiritually. I felt like I could get no rest, find no peace.

When we get to this place, the enemy targets our "soul." Soul, in this sense, is defined as our mind, our will, and our emotions. If the adversary can twist up your mind so you can't think straight, he'll do it. If he can get you all emotional so you make a bad decision, he'll do it. If he can break down your will power, he will.

Jesus is at this place in Gethsemane. The place of "crushing olives." And He's using His life as an example of our personal life pressures. He realizes what is happening to Him, so He prays, three times. Perhaps you have heard this prayer before: "My Father, if it is possible, may this cup be taken from me. Yet, not as I will, but as you will" (Matthew 26:39 NIV).

It is vital that we remember that it is the Son of God praying here, the One who said, "If you've seen me, you have seen the Father." He's now under intense pressure. The adversary is trying to "break Him," but the enemy is not going to succeed. *Jesus never broke!* Still, the pressure was on Him. Even the physical setting is a place where things are crushed. Jesus is in that moment, and He's setting an example for you and me. He is telling us, "You will come to a breaking point, and you will need to decide how to respond."

Breaking points are emotional, but we should not respond to them based on our feelings. Our feelings are simply an option to the truth that God has designed to set us free! Choosing our feelings over truth is how we end up following our own way rather than God's way. Jesus shows us how to break through without breaking. He says, "Not my will . . . ."

Jesus understands Whom He is praying to. Remember, He is using His personal life and this situation to teach what we must do when we experience the pressures of life. He's praying to His Father, Who loves Him. He's praying to a Father Who loves and forgives, and Who's full of mercy and grace; Who saves, delivers, transforms, and has all power.

BREAKING POINTS ARE EMOTIONAL, BUT WE SHOULD NOT RESPOND TO THEM BASED ON OUR EMOTIONS.

Jesus is praying to His Father because He is at a pressure point, just as many people reading this book are at a pressure point: The pressure to have an affair. The pressure to cheat on the job. The pressure to lie. The pressure to compromise. The pressure to be offended. The pressure to be angry, or unforgiving.

So many people claim, "I love God, but I'm going to do whatever I want. I'll ask Him to forgive me later. I'll get back with God as soon as I'm done."

But this is a lack of sincerity and honesty. In fact, it's nothing but a religious "con game."

Jesus doesn't take this option—the easy way out. Even though He was battling intense pressure and despair, He follows the

Father's will. He broke through the pressure. He broke through for all of humanity. He showed us how to do it. The key? Total surrender to God's will and God's Word! I know it sounds easy, but it's also not as simple as it sounds. Total surrender. Surrender doesn't require perfection, but it does require devotion.

The disciples, on the other hand, did not have a breakthrough. Some of them fell asleep. Some of them ran away. One of them betrayed Jesus. Another disciple made excuses and even denied Jesus. So when it came to surrender, every one of His 12 disciples failed.

Jesus responded with compassion and mercy toward His disciples. This is another lesson for us. Our God is merciful. He never writes us off. He's always there for us if only we will turn to Him.

This is one reason why it's important to have a daily devotion time. We need to read God's Word daily, because I promise you that the Father wants to speak to you every day from His Word.

We all go through those "oil press" times. Maybe you are in the middle of one right now. I encourage you to let God's Word be your standard, especially when life is heavy on you. You might think that you'll get some relief if you collapse under the weight of despair or temptation or whatever. It's tempting to say, "I'm going to give in, just to get some relief. I can't bear this weight anymore."

However, we should remember what is on the other side of a decision like that: misery, disappointment, guilt, or a loss of direction in life.

It's also important to realize that the enemy doesn't necessarily want us to flip out in the face of crisis and suddenly give up on Jesus. Most of us probably wouldn't do that. Instead, it's the small steps that lead us away. The little things we know we shouldn't do, but keep doing anyway. As C.S. Lewis warns in his book "The Screwtape Letters," "The safest road to Hell is the gradual one—the gentle slope, soft underfoot, without sudden turning, without milestones, without signposts."

Many Christians don't consciously try to do something bad, but many fail to make the right decisions. And the results of this mistake are equally as bad.

As I close this chapter, I want to speak primarily to the young in the Lord. In other words, Christians who are still growing and developing in how to be led by the Spirit of God, how to hear the voice of God, and how to make critical decisions in life: faith decisions. (Come to think of it, in light of eternity, aren't we all young?) So, I guess I am talking to everybody.

James 1:22 (Amplified Bible, Classic Edition) urges us, "Be doers of the Word [obey the message], and not merely listeners to it, betraying yourselves [into deception by reasoning contrary to the Truth].

With this verse in mind, let me offer some advice on walking out your Christian life. I wouldn't presume to tell you that God cannot speak to you. I know He can. But as a pastor, I sometimes hear people say, "I heard thunder, and God spoke to me and told me to go minister in the Himalayas!"

That probably was not God. That was probably emotions. Sometimes, we believe more in our emotions than we believe in God's Word.

I empathize with this tendency. I am a very passionate person—very emotional. Emotions are good, and they have a purpose. After all, God created us with emotions. Prior to being born again, the primary way that we make decisions is by our senses. Yet, Romans 8:5-8 NKJV says this about our senses: "For those who live according the flesh set their mind on the things of the flesh, but those who live according to the Sprit, the things of the Spirit. For to be carnally minded is death, but to be spiritually minded is life and peace. Because the carnal mind is enmity against God; for it is not subject to the law of God, nor indeed can be. So then, those who are in the flesh cannot please God." What Paul explains here is that we are to be led by the Holy Spirit and not merely our senses. This is a "new creation in Christ" reality. In my case, I can tend to get all fired up and emotional. This is not always a good thing, especially if it's not balanced with truth, because it can lead to extreme reactions or bad decision-making. The Bible does not say your emotions or feelings or senses will set you free. It teaches us that the truth will set us free. (See John 8:32.)

When I first became a Christian, God really instructed me to follow Him by what He said, not by my emotions. This is called the walk of faith. Paul told us to walk by faith and not by sight or our senses. (See 2 Corinthians 5:7.) I, like every other Christian, needed to retrain myself to make this change. In my life, I was very emotionally driven. I had lived my entire life on emotions—how things felt or seemed. I didn't know how to truly love God, because love for God requires *more* than emotion. Loving God can *involve* emotions, but it's more about trusting God's Word and what He says. The Holy Spirit will confirm God's Word and teach us.

God began to teach me what I am sharing with you now. He began to show me how to be a "doer of the Word." He helped me understand, "If you love me, keep my commands" (John 14:15 NIV). Obedience and application to what God's Word says ought to be our standard, not our emotions. This was a revelation to me. Previously, I used to think, "If

LOVE FOR GOD REQUIRES MORE THAN EMOTION.

I cannot feel God, I guess I don't love Him. And if I don't feel Him, He doesn't love me either."

I worried that something was wrong in my relationship with

Christ. This created doubt, fear, and unbelief. I was an emotional basket case—up and down and all around.

And then the Lord directed me to the Scripture:

> *"Be doers of the Word [obey the message], and not merely listeners to it, betraying yourselves [into deception by reasoning contrary to the truth"* (James 1:22 AMPC).

Yes, reasoning is important to us. There is a place for it. But reason is not faith, and faith is not reason. We must live our life stories by the truth. Jesus said in John 17:17, "Thy word is truth" (KJV). So it's not just about the facts of life. Let me explain what I mean. Facts are circumstances. You

TRUTH IS BIGGER THAN THE FACTS. FACTS DON'T SET YOU FREE. TRUTH DOES.

can, in fact, have a problem. Perhaps you don't have enough money in your wallet. Or maybe you have pain somewhere in your body. It can even be a fact that certain people do not like you. Or that you, in fact, are offended, hurt, or unforgiving toward someone for what he or she did to you. That would be unfortunate, but facts are real. We should not deny them.

But truth is bigger than the facts. Facts don't set you free. Truth does. The Bible assures us that we shall know the truth, and the truth shall set us free. But if we don't know the truth of God's Word, how is it going to set us free? Some Christians make Jesus sound like He's "Casper, the friendly ghost." He's just going to float in and do everything for us. Fix all of the problems in our life stories.

Here is how the New King James version renders James 1:22: "Be doers of the word, and not hearers only, deceiving yourselves." We have to be aware of this self-deception. My emotions can go contrary to the truth. My feelings can be calling out, "I don't want to forgive that person! I want to stay bitter!" or "I want to stay angry at my wife," or "I want to be upset at my children (or my parents)."

Our feelings can also tell us, "You are a failure. You are a loser. That's why you feel like a loser!" These feelings can be powerful. Again, I am not saying they don't exist. They are facts of life. But the truth, not the facts, sets us free.

Jesus says, "Whom the son sets free is free indeed." The Bible gives us God's promises, and every one of God's promises is truth. They are God's "yes and amen!" (See 2 Corinthians 1:20.) The Bible says that "the joy of the Lord is your strength" (Nehemiah 8:10 NIV). The Bible promises, "You will keep him in perfect peace, whose mind is stayed on You, Because he trusts in You" (Isaiah 26:3 NKJV). It's possible to pray and not feel like anything has changed. Keep praying anyway. You must pray to change things.

God's Word promises us, "Now this is the confidence that we have in Him, that if we ask anything according to His will, He hears us. And if we know that He hears us, whatever we ask, we know that we have the petitions that we have asked of Him" (1 John 5:14-15 NKJV). The Bible also tells us, regardless of how young a Christian we are, once we receive the Lord we are a "new creation." (See 2 Corinthians 5:17.) Further, you and I are the righteousness of God in Christ Jesus (2 Corinthians 5:21). We must rely on Scriptures like these, not our feelings. Because it's possible that a minister will lay hands on you, pray for you, and you'll think, "I don't feel anything, pastor."

Well, you don't have to feel anything. You just have to receive by faith. It's not about the feeling. It's about how God says He ministers to people. Hebrews 6:1-3 talks about the laying on of hands in the time of ministry. It's about the blessing or the encouragement or the love you have received.

As we seek to change our stories, we are sometimes our own worst enemies. We think we know better than God. Well, we don't. God is the creator; we are the created. But we develop what I call the Spirit of Familiarity. That is, we have become too familiar with life as we have always known it to be. That's why we can get stuck and cannot see beyond our current circumstances, culture, conflicts, or negative conditions.

But God can see beyond all of our negativity, difficulty,

trouble, and problems. That's why He tells us to trust Him with all of our hearts. (See Proverbs 3:5-7.) He is a God of faith. He requires you and me—His people—to trust Him! So be encouraged. God truly wants you to take on the challenge of changing your story. All that you have experienced so far is not all there is. God has so much more for you! Today He's telling you: Forget those things that are behind and reach forward to those things which are ahead. (See Philippians 3:13.)

Please read these next words thoughtfully: You cannot conquer what you do not confront, and you cannot confront what you do not identify.

As we think about making our stories better than ever, God is asking us to identify where we *are*, so that we can move forward to God's destination for us. As a pastor, I frequently remind my congregation, "God knows where we are. God knows where He wants us to be. And only God knows how to get us there." In other words, God is the author of our life stories. If we follow His lead, He will guide us through a better story than we can even imagine.

YOU CANNOT CONQUER WHAT YOU DO NOT CONFRONT, AND YOU CANNOT CONFRONT WHAT YOU DO NOT IDENTIFY.

God can take us from breaking point to breaking through . . . and beyond!

13

"Be" The Story

Don't trade your story for someone else's. Don't waste your life trying to keep up with anyone else. God has written a unique and valuable story for each of us, but when we don't take care of what God has given us, it's so easy to want someone else's life. Your story was designed to have value and purpose, but you must first value your own story. God has already included in your story all of the elements you need to live an extraordinary life. You simply need to "be" the story He's given you, to live it out to its fullest potential. Own your own story.

In the book of Timothy, Paul is talking to one of his students, a disciple named Timothy. He is mentoring Timothy as a young man on how to be an effective example and influence for Christ. Paul tells Timothy, "Let no one despise your youth, but be an example to the believers in word, in conduct, in love, in spirit, in faith, in purity" (1 Timothy 4:12 NKJV).

Here, Paul is advising a younger man, but there is more than one way to be young. Perhaps you are young in your faith toward God, or young in a leadership position. Whatever the case, don't let anyone despise your youth or lack of experience as you live out your story. In fact, Paul's advice to Timothy is on how to build a strong, productive, powerful, and influential story that will demonstrate what it means to be the story, the salt and light in a dark world. He helps Timothy understand what God requires of him—and how he can build a foundation of leadership and influence. Paul encourages Timothy to be the story in several areas.

Let's consider each one and how we can apply this advice to our lives.

First, we should set an example **"in word."** Let's look at two aspects of this advice. We should take care with the way we use God's Word in our lives. That is, how do we apply God's Word to the life situations we face? In the Bible, James tells us to "be doers of the Word" (James 1:22).

The second aspect of this advice is *how* we speak, the actual words we use. Are our words filled with hope, encouragement, and edification? Paul notes, "Don't use foul or abusive language. Let everything you say be good and helpful, so that your words will be an encouragement to those who hear them" (See Ephesians 4:29 NLT.) Our words can carry faith or fear. They can be uplifting or downright discouraging. They can be full of hope or leave a person feeling helpless.

How is your speech these days? Solomon said, "The tongue has the power of life and death" (Proverbs 18:21 NIV) and "You have been trapped by what you said, ensnared by the words of your mouth" (Proverbs 6:2 NIV). Our prayer should be, "Help me eliminate words that are ineffective or negative. Help me avoid words that hurt others. Help my words to be wise and encouraging."

David prayed, "Set a guard, O LORD, over my mouth; Keep watch over the door of my lips" (Psalms 141:3 NKJV). David understood the power of words. It was David who taught his son Solomon how to use words wisely.

Second, we should set an example **"in conduct"** both public and private. Our conduct is a direct reflection of our character. A good question to ask yourself is "Who am I when nobody's looking?" In other words, is your character compartmentalized or is it consistent?

Now, I am not talking about being perfect. I am speaking about being an example. Living for Christ is not about "Sunday Church" only. Our entire lives should be exemplary.

Paul wrote to the Corinthians, "You yourselves are our letter, written on our hearts, known and read by everyone" (2 Corinthians 3:2 NIV). For instance, in our relationships with our significant others, we need to mind how we're handling our business. This means, young people, don't take advantage of your boyfriend or girlfriend. Don't have sex outside of marriage, even if all your friends are doing it. You'll end up hurting yourself and the other person too. If you mess up, God will still love you, but He won't endorse that kind of behavior. It will hinder the blessing and favor of God on your life.

The Bible teaches us to live pure lives (See 1 Thessalonians 4:1-4) and that we ought to know how to keep ourselves pure. This is not religious perfection—it's called purity.

We don't become pure to win God's love. The Bible states God loved us while we were yet sinners. (See Romans 5:8.) Living worldly because everyone else is doing it doesn't make you hip, fashionable, popular, or fulfilled. It will eventually leave a person hurting, frustrated, and unfulfilled.

Don't look at what others are doing. Focus on who you are living for. Jesus said no man can serve two masters. Living fleshly or worldly will eventually cause a major disruption. Live for Christ. Be committed. Don't be double-minded. Then His presence, power, peace, and prosperity will follow you all the days of your life.

Disobeying God in this area of your life leads to frustration. It keeps your story from being all it can be.

So often, good conduct is about restraint. Again, it's about who you are when no one is looking. That is a true test of who you are. Another true test is how you handle yourself with difficult people, people who might treat you badly. You can't respond by barking right back at them. And don't let your life be consumed by others' negativity. Your conduct must reflect trusting God and loving people. If you are frustrated by these people, why would you want to behave just as they do?

Jesus tells us to turn the other cheek. That means more than just offering your other cheek for someone to smack. Truly turning the other cheek means acting completely different from how your antagonist is treating you, which means that although life hurts, you don't have to live hurt or offended.

Third, we should set an example **"in love."** And this includes loving the unlovely. I have news for you, if you don't already know this: You are going to encounter unlovely people. Maybe you had a recent encounter? These people are not easy to love, but that is what we are commanded to do. What should this love look like?

> GOOD CONDUCT IS ABOUT RESTRAINT. IT'S ABOUT WHO YOU ARE WHEN NO ONE IS LOOKING.

When Paul mentored Timothy to be an example of God's love, he pointed to Jesus as the ultimate example.

Jesus was and is the love of the Father manifest on earth. He is our model. You may have people you call role models and mentors in life, but there is no one greater than Jesus Himself. He revealed the difference between law-religion and a loving relationship. The religious leaders of His day had been law-bound and set in their minds on how to treat people.

They thought that their religious ways and practices were without fault. That is, until Jesus came. In Matthew 5, Jesus taught that it was all about loving people back to life. He said we are blessed (and we bless others) when we are meek, merciful, pure in heart, and when we are peace-makers. He said we should not be angry with one another or say hateful things.

We should reconcile our differences and settle our disputes. Near the end of Matthew 5, Jesus instructed, "You have heard that it was said, 'Love your neighbor and hate your enemy.' But I tell you, love your enemies and pray for those who persecute you, that you may be children of your Father in heaven" (Matthew 5:43-45 NIV).

Here is one of the Bible's most famous passages on love:

Living in Love

Love endures long and is patient and kind; love never is envious nor boils over with jealousy, is not boastful or vainglorious, does not display itself haughtily.

It is not conceited (arrogant and inflated with

pride); it is not rude (unmannerly) and does not act unbecomingly. Love (God's love in us) does not insist on its own rights or its own way, for it is not self-seeking; it is not touchy or fretful or resentful; it takes no account of the evil done to it [it pays no attention to a suffered wrong].

It does not rejoice at injustice and unrighteousness, but rejoices when right and truth prevail. Love bears up under anything and everything that comes, is ever ready to believe the best of every person, its hopes are fadeless under all circumstances, and it endures everything [without weakening].

Love never fails [never fades out or becomes obsolete or comes to an end].

1 Corinthians 13: 4-8a, AMP Classic

Keep this Scripture in mind, especially as you encounter those who do not know Christ. God does not say, "You know what? It's OK. You don't have to love that non-Christian. You can be as mean as you want."

Are you kidding me? God's standard is not based on how we feel. It's based on His Word. His standard for our conduct does not change. Some of us reading what Paul wrote may say, "Can anybody fulfill that standard?" Well, nobody's perfect, but in our devotion for Christ, that's what we should set our standard to be—His Word. You see, without God's setting the boundaries of how to love people, there would be no standards. Behavior would be subject to one's mood or feelings or whatever.

Fourth, we should set an example in **"in spirit"** or attitude. The Bible tells us to have that same attitude Christ had. (See Philippians 2:5.)

Here's a question for you: How is your attitude these days? Are you positive, uplifting, and encouraging? Faith-building? Hope-inspiring? Destiny-motivating to yourself and others? Or are you depressed all the time? Are you bummed out because of how people are treating you? Upset and irritated because of life challenges? Faithless? Doubting? Is the Holy Spirit evident in your attitude?

Of course, none of us sets a perfect example all the time. Still, if we commit to a standard, we should work to meet that standard. Not a standard set by fashion icons, reality TV shows, the rich and famous, or the popular pundits of our day. But a standard called the Bible and its promises. We should keep the standard in mind as we interact with family, friends, co-workers, and everyone else. God's not saying, "You must be perfect or nothing's going to work in your life."

No. God simply wants us to strive to keep the standard, even when life's pressures come at us. We should have the right attitude, speak the right words, and choose the right actions. We should love people even when they are being difficult.

We should walk by faith and not by . . . what? Sight!

Fifth, we should set an example by **"walking by faith."** Remember our story of Jesus in the Garden of Gethsemane? He felt distressed and full of sorrow. But He did not submit to that sorrow. The Bible promises that if we resist the devil, he will flee. So resist him. Humbly submit yourself to God. Let faith guide you, above anything else.

Sixth, we should set an example **"in purity."** God wants us to be pure in our motives. Do you know someone who lives an impure life? Does he expose himself to unclean things all of the time? Is it any wonder that people like this have impure thoughts? Is it any wonder that this impurity pollutes their life stories?

The Bible tells us that "the whole world is under the control of the evil one" (I John 5:19 NIV)—and that we are to be in the world but not *OF* the world. This means we must pursue purity and avoid impurity.

Impurity is about the lust of the eyes, the lust of the flesh, and the pride of life. (See 1 John 2:16.) I am not trying to give you "hell fire and brimstone," but an impure life will never give you the peace, prosperity, presence, power, or passion that you or someone you know is looking for. Never. We see this with Lot and his family in the Old Testament. Impurity affects your soul.

That's what our adversary, Satan, targets: your soul. (Your soul, in this context, means your mind, will, and emotions.)

How are we targeted? Through our eyes and ears, which are the gateways that lead to our heart. What we see and hear in our surroundings can influence us. Let's read how an impure environment affected Lot: "And He rescued righteous Lot, greatly worn out and distressed by the wanton ways of the ungodly and lawless" (2 Peter 2:7 AMP Classic).

Of course, we all stumble, but that doesn't necessarily mean we are impure. But it's worth keeping a close eye on your thoughts, attitudes, and speech, all the same. This is how we avoid becoming "greatly worn out and distressed" like Lot.

Jesus says to us, "If you love Me, keep My Commandments" (John 14:15 NKJV). When you follow God's word, you will be fruitful in your lives. You will see His blessings on your life story as never before.

Word. Conduct. Love. Spirit. Faith. Purity. These were Paul's elementary principals to Timothy. These were the keys to leading by example. If you will apply these insights, by faith, to your life, God, by the Holy Spirit, will immediately begin to work. You will find God building your life story His way. His Word has power to transform your life and will set you free! His Word promises you that. I have seen it happen in a multitude of lives.

It begins with your decision. As Pastor Cesar Castellanos often says: "If I change, everything will change."

But, you must decide. Decide to make God's Word the final authority in your life. Make it numero uno. Do the simple things, like your daily devotions. That's how you ought to begin every day—having time with Him. God's Word is God's voice, ready to speak to you daily. It's simple and easy. Just open the Bible, and the Holy Spirit will begin to work with you right where you are! Ask God to speak to you. He will, because the Holy Spirit is very personal. He wants to speak with you every day. He will direct you and empower you. God wants to prove Himself to you, show you how real He is. God is as real as the ground you stand on. Yes, that real.

> ## "IF I CHANGE, EVERYTHING WILL CHANGE."
>
> PASTOR CESAR CASTELLANOS

With that truth in mind, let's close this chapter in prayer:

> Father, we come to You as the God who changes our story. It is so good to know that we're in constant change, constantly being worked on, and constantly being loved by You. Thank You for letting us know that when the pressure of life is on, we don't have to be a statistic and break down. Rather, in the name of Jesus, we can break through! You're so committed to us and to our ever-developing story. That commitment is seen

on the cross of Calvary. There's no doubt how much You love us. There's no questioning Your commitment to see us live an effective, powerful, and productive life. There's not a person reading this book whom You've ever, ever written off. Father, no matter what we've done, either intentionally or by mistake, Your forgiveness, mercy, and tender loving-kindnesses are renewed every day—and we say thank You. Thank You for Your grace. Thank You for the wonderful work of the Holy Spirit in our lives. Thank You for seeing us through the eyes of faith. Thank You for breathing life into everyone reading this book. Thank You for being with us.

Even now in this moment, Your mercies are evident in our midst. Your healing grace and healing power are present. Lord, there's just no stopping Your work. And we refuse to put any limits, any boundaries, any borders on what You want to do in any person's life. That work is eternal. We also commit to applying your Word in our life. We too, by the work of the Holy Spirit, choose to be an example to all believers in word, conduct, love, spirit, faith, and in purity by the grace of God.

Father, we stand in awe of how much You love us. Even when we know we've fallen short, there

You are to pick us up. You put our feet back on the rock. Please give us a new song to sing. A song of praise, a song of joy. I pray for people's peace. I pray for their joy to reach a new level, in every life.

Father, I declare right now that no weapon forming against any person reading this book shall prosper against him or her. Every word that the enemy has tried to bring up against their lives, concerning their past or present, is broken in the name of Jesus.

I declare that there is no condemnation for those who are in Christ Jesus, Who frees us from the law of sin and death. We are no longer bound, no longer slaves to sin. We can live that new life. I pray that people will break free and commit to do Your will as You reveal it to them.

Finally, may everyone reading these words know what a powerful purpose You have for him or her.

Amen.

14

We're Gonna Save
the World Tonight

Never undervalue your ability to make a difference in this world. There are reasons why God wants to change your story. First, certainly, to benefit you. He wants you well, whole, healed, and living healthy in every category of your personal life. God cares about you! But there's a second reason: For the sake of others. That's right. I know you may have doubts about your ability, but God does not. As a leader, you are anointed, appointed, and, as I like to say, "deputized, authorized, and energized." Oh, that carries some biblical substance to it. Paul teaches all believers where his ability comes from in 2 Corinthians 3:3-4 (AMP Classic):

> *"You show and make obvious that you are a letter*
> *from Christ delivered by us, not written with ink*

but with [the] Spirit of [the] living God, not on tablets of stone but on tablets of human hearts. Such is the reliance and confidence that we have through Christ toward and with reference to God."

You have the power to change your story in order to help change the story of others—because your ability is His ability. The Bible even defines you as a dispenser of God's salvation in Christ Jesus by the Holy Spirit. (See 2 Corinthians 3:6.) It's obvious that this is a word of grace and of His amazing, unconditional love. Your life does not only have ability and dispensing power, but influence. Jesus told us to be the salt and light of the world. That we are not to be hidden under a basket, but as the church, we are to be a city on a hill. Matthew 5:13-16 (NKJV) assures us:

"You are the salt of the earth; but if the salt loses its flavor, how shall it be seasoned? It is then good for nothing but to be thrown out and trampled underfoot by men. You are the light of the world. A city that is set on a hill cannot be hidden. Nor do they light a lamp and put it under a basket, but on a lampstand, and it gives light to all who are in the house. Let your light so shine before men, that they may see your good works and glorify your Father in heaven."

So what Jesus is saying is that He's wanting your life to reflect His life-transforming work in you "seen" by all people! One day, while I was studying the power of His ability to change any person's story, I heard this phrase well up in my heart: "I can change the story of a city by changing the story of one person at a time!"

God was speaking of the power and ability that one person has to influence the world. It's in total alignment with what Jesus told the church when He said "Be a city on a hill." I know the value of community. The value of a team, a group, a gathering. But He was also speaking of your value as *one*! One living for Him. When a person like you reading this book seeks God with a hunger, that person is positioned to do exploits. That's why, with a deep-hearted conviction, wherever I go and whenever the opportunity arises, I shout it from the rooftops:

> **GOD CAN CHANGE THE STORY OF A CITY BY CHANGING THE STORY OF ONE PERSON AT A TIME.**

> Be encouraged. I believe by the grace of God you are that "one person" and this is your time.

A few years ago I heard a song that really resonated in my soul. It is titled *"Save the World"* by a group called Swedish House Mafia:

Into the streets, we're coming down

We never sleep, never get tired

Through urban fields, and suburban life

Turn the crowd up now, we'll never back down

Shoot down a skyline, watch it in primetime

Turn up the love now, listen up now, turn up
the love.

Who's gonna save the world tonight?

Who's gonna bring it back to life?

We're gonna make it, you and I

We're gonna save the world tonight.

In hearing these words, it's as if I sense a "tag of the Holy Spirit" upon my heart. (Tags are things God uses to get my attention.) These lyrics motivate me and challenge me at the same time. They pose powerful questions: Who is going to make a difference? Who is going to take on the challenge facing the church?

By now, you probably know that when I say "church," I am not talking about a building, but about "a people." Not just any group of people, found on any corner of the street, but people who, like you and me, have been born again—the church!

Now, I am not saying that we are saviors of the world. That title belongs to Jesus alone. But as we've read, He's given us an ability and sufficiency to dispense Christ's salvation—to share the good news of the Gospel and hold forth the word of life to our generation. Again, to be the salt and light of the world. His Holy Spirit lives in us, and He does His work through people:

> *"[Not in your own strength] for it is God Who is all the while effectually at work in you [energizing and creating in you the power and desire], both to will and to work for His good pleasure and satisfaction and delight" [Philippians 2:13 AMP Classic].*

Jesus is the ultimate story changer, and He compels His church to follow Him and allow His Spirit to work in us to change the stories of others. Jesus can change any person's story. The Bible proves this over and over.

One reason I love the Bible is that it's so real. If you made an accurate movie based on the Bible, it would have to be rated "R." I don't mean "risqué," but real. The Bible's stories don't present a perfect picture of perfect people we could never emulate. Instead, we see a perfect God working with very imperfect people, through faith in His grace. These people are being perfected day by day. He heals their lives. He walks beside them on their journeys.

Earlier in the book, we talked about King David. Although one of the greater kings Israel ever had—with conquests and victories and triumphs that boggle the mind—David had his imperfections. David, as you probably know, committed adultery, lied, cheated, and also was a murderer. Yet God once called David "a man after My own heart." Like you, I wonder, "How was this possible?" (I mean, sometimes I do the simplest of mistakes—like argue with my spouse. I give a person an unkind gesture. I act inappropriately, become irritated or disturbed. And I can sense God's displeasure in my actions. I can sense my need for repentance.) But when it comes to David, historians say it took him a year to 18 months to actually repent before Nathan the prophet.

"How could this be?" you might ask. The same way it can be for you. That's my answer. The same way it can be for anyone.

God does not want to rip up and throw away the pages of anyone's story. As David marveled, "God made my life complete when I placed all the pieces before Him. . . . God rewrote the text of my life when I opened the book of my heart. . . ." (2 Samuel 22:21, 25 MSG).

When you read a powerful novel, the words create images in your mind. And when it comes to our own stories, we all have images that haunt us. Images that we fear will scar or define our lives forever. We feel stuck in our own story.

When we feel this way, we need to remember David and how God rewrote the text of his life. Just imagine how God can rewrite your text! Then keep imagining. Imagine how God can change all kinds of lives, one person at a time—one person like you!

Why was it possible for David, and why do I know it's possible for you? You see, David didn't get a "special pass." He didn't take some special potion, nor did God have a different set of standards. David repented. In other words, he surrendered and asked God to forgive him. But don't think that for that a year or more that he, too, wasn't dealing with guilt, condemnation, and hidden shame. God doesn't play favorites. He is no respecter of persons. That's why David's life is a great example of God changing a story. Once Nathan revealed to David what God had revealed to him, David did not try to use his title and position against Nathan. He did not make excuses. He didn't deny anything. He only accepted the truth. This is why the Bible calls David "a man after God's own heart."

As you ponder these possibilities, it's time to review a few key truths we have explored so far in this book:

1. Everyone has a story.

2. Every story is important to God.

3. Every story that everyone has is not the story that everyone wants.

4. Jesus is the story changer. He can change any-one's story for the better.

5. God can change the story of a city (and beyond) by changing the story of one person at a time. I would love for YOU to be that person!

This is why I say to you, again, what God revealed to me: "God can change the story of a city by changing the story of one person at a time." You are that "one *person,*" and this is your time!

I want to make sure that you understand that God changes stories through a personal relationship with Jesus Christ. We can change our stories when we encounter Christ and have an up-close experience with Him. I'm talking about going beyond emotion to conviction to being true disciples.

The classic writer Oswald Chambers noted that the word "Christian" appeared in his Bible only three times. But the word "disciple": a whopping 269 times.

So how does God change the story of one person at a time? Jesus told His followers to go into the world and "make disciples of all the nations" (Matthew 28:19 NKJV). As we have learned, a disciple is more than a church attender. A disciple is a life-long learner and a Christ-follower. A true disciple is a new breed of people—people committed to following God wherever He leads.

Greg Laurie once said, "Every disciple is a believer, but not every believer is a disciple."

That's a great quote. When God changes a person's story, He changes a person's heart. God gives uncommon power and an uncommon dream for us to live out. I have no doubt that God will provide all this to every person reading this book. Will every person accept? That's another matter. But the truth remains: God wants you to experience all He has for you!

In the book of Acts, chapter 10, we rejoin the continuing saga of Peter, Jesus' disciple. It's about 10 years after Jesus has risen from the dead and ascended into heaven. God shows up and has an encounter with Peter. I'm like Peter in so many ways: I don't get it the first time, the second time, or even the third time!

A DISCIPLE IS A LIFE-LONG LEARNER AND A CHRIST-FOLLOWER.

You see, Peter's peers have been asking him, "Peter, you had an encounter with God! What happened? What did He tell you? Did He really tell you that you could kill and eat *any* kind of food—animal, bird, or even reptile! Food that is common and not kosher!"

Peter replies that he has been told, "What God has cleansed, you must not call common" (Acts 11:9b NKJV).

Common, of course, means average, typical, or undistinguished. A common person might be someone considered unremarkable in any way.

You might consider yourself to be common. Plain Jane or Average Joe. I am here to tell you that when God changes your life, He does not leave you plain, Jane. He changes your life. He gives you an uncommon life in Christ, an uncommon power through the Holy Spirit, and an uncommon dream from God the Father. Literally, the Good News of the Gospel is that when you ask Jesus into your heart as your Lord and Savior (according to Romans 10:9-10), He promises to give you a new identity, a new ability, and a new destiny! An uncommon life, filled with an uncommon power, to live out an uncommon dream—the Father's Dream for your life.

Who can have his or her life changed this way? I'll tell you . . . Whosoever.

Matthew 10:32 (KJV) assures us,

> *"Whosoever therefore shall confess me before men, him will I confess also before my Father which is in heaven."*

"Whosoever" is you and I, the people. The people who make up the church. I have said it before, and I'll say it again: I honestly believe that the church can change the story of a city by changing the story of one person at a time.

We get a picture of how this change happens from the book of Judges, chapter 6. Here we find the story of the nation of

Israel. Verse 1 tells us, "The Israelites did evil in the eyes of the Lord, and for seven years he gave them into the hands of the Midianites" (NIV).

I want you to understand that God delivered the children of Israel into enemy hands because of the choices they made. God didn't randomly decide to let something bad happen to His people. He does not work that way.

Let me illustrate how God works. Imagine that the Israelites lived in an area marked by highly acidic rain. God provides them a huge umbrella and tells them, "As long as you stay under this umbrella, you will have My protection. You will be blessed."

In this story, God is not bringing the acid rain upon the people. He's telling them how to stay safe. He's saying, "You are covered as long as you obey Me and live in covenant with Me."

But what happens the moment someone leaves the protection of the umbrella? The acid rain starts to eat away his forehead! He shouldn't blame God. He should have thought twice before making a bad decision. God is for us, not against us.

Now, let's get back to our story in Judges 6. The Israelites were delivered into the hands of the Midianites for seven years. They suffered poor living conditions, including dens and cages they made for themselves to live in. When the Israelites grew crops, the Midianites invaded and ruined everything. The same thing happened with the sheep, cattle, and other livestock the

Israelites tried to raise. Israel was left with no sustenance. These people were impoverished.

Not surprisingly, they cried out to the Lord.

It's important to remember that the Israelites suffered at Midianite hands for seven years. Not seven weeks or even seven months. Can you imagine trying to make a life for yourself and your family for seven years—only to see your work ravaged time after time?

Remember what we learned earlier: What you tolerate, you authorize to stay in your life.

The people of Israel were attacked on many fronts, just as we are today. Our enemy's attacks might take the form of depression, emotional upheaval, or confusion. The attack can even be economic. But we stay stuck in our misery because we don't ask the Lord for help. We blame other people for our problems. Or we blame God.

EXCUSES ARE THE CRUTCHES OF THE UNCOMMITTED.

Do you know someone who is always depressed and hopeless—and blames various people for the state he or she is in? People like this have a disease I call "excusitis." It's an epidemic in modern society.

At my church, I tell the people all of the time, "Excuses are the crutches of the uncommitted." People who are not truly committed to God fail to approach Him when they need Him. In times of trouble, they run away from God. Or they get angry at Him and turn their backs. So they separate themselves from the One who can deliver them and sustain them in any area of life.

Like the Israelites, they wallow in misery. I have to shake my head when I think of these people, living in poverty and growing more bitter all the time. They probably blamed each other for their troubles. And these were people who knew their long history as children of God. They knew how God had delivered them time and again, all the way back to the days of Moses! They knew about the miracles God performed for them.

These Israelites remind me of modern people, people who know a few things about Jesus and even attend church once in a while. But when trouble comes, they don't seek Jesus for help. They continue in their sadness and bitterness. Their hearts become increasingly hard and cold.

But it's never too late.

Let's rejoin the Israelites, after those seven grueling years: "When the Israelites cried out to the LORD because of Midian, he sent them a prophet who said, 'This is what the LORD, the God of Israel, says: I brought you up out of Egypt, out of the land of slavery'" (Judges 6:7-8 NIV).

Let's make sure we understand the impact of these verses. The moment the people cried out to God, He began to work on their behalf.

When the Bible talks about the people crying out, it doesn't mean a bunch of "boo-hooing." These people are returning to God. They are saying, "We know we have moved away from You, but we need You. We can't make it on our own. Please help us!" They are genuinely repenting.

And repentance always brings rescue. When I humbly approach God on His throne, He is not hard of hearing. He hears and responds. Please believe me: God has not forgotten you. He has not abandoned your story. He does not leave you miserable. Heaven moves when God hears the heart of a repentant person.

HEAVEN MOVES WHEN GOD HEARS THE HEART OF A REPENTANT PERSON.

In Judges, God responds right away by sending a prophet. A prophet to help His people.

Sometimes we have trouble listening to "prophets," to people who can lead us and help us grow. Do you know someone whose attitude is "Don't tell me what to do! Don't tell me how to live!"

It's hard for people like this to become a disciple, and that's one of the toughest tests of our character: Can we be disciples?

Most people are not disciples simply because they don't want to be. They don't want to be told how to live. They don't want to learn from someone else. They think they can figure out everything for themselves. When I encounter people like this, I want to say, "Really? How long are you going to keep pounding your fists against a brick wall before you figure out that there is a better way?"

Jesus challenged His followers to go out and make disciples of all nations. And to make someone else a disciple, you must be one yourself. Think about it: How could you disciple someone if you have not been discipled yourself?

I do not have the right to speak into anybody's life until I have given someone that same right to speak into my life. This is true for all of us.

Sometimes, a disciple has to hear hard truths. In our story from Judges, the prophet reminds the Israelites that they failed to obey God's voice. That's what got them into trouble. The prophet also helps them understand that God did not cause their trouble. They are the ones who "left the covering of the umbrella." God is not the problem. He is the solution.

This prophet is a heaven-sent source of correction and direction. But the people will need to listen to him. They will need to let him speak into their lives. This is a vital message for us today. If we fail to be good disciples and let someone guide us, we will not get to where we want to be. We must become fully devoted followers of Christ. We must allow the person discipling us to help set our lives in order.

The people of Israel did this. They started by repenting and returning to God.

That was a great start, but it was only a start. The day someone becomes a Christian—or rededicates his life to Jesus—everything does not change immediately. Like a newborn deer, we don't walk or run perfectly the moment after we are born. Learning how to treat people and how to live God's way takes time. There are things to be learned. (Always remember, a disciple is a learner.)

Have you heard someone say, "Well, I went to the altar when the pastor called me, so I guess I'm a disciple now"?

When I hear this, I respond, "I am glad you went forward. That was a very real experience. But it's only the beginning of your journey. To continue the journey, to grow as a Christian, you must be willing to be discipled—even if you're one of those people who don't like taking direction from anyone."

When we are willing to be disciples, the church can change the story of a city, and beyond, one person at a time. Changing the world starts with one. Let's all be willing to be that "one!"

15

Your Now Step

Jesus is the Story Changer. Do not make the mistake of thinking this answer is overly simplistic. You see, changing one's story is not merely an intellectual endeavor based on human wisdom or worldly experience. Nor is it about the latest "sound bites" that tend to tickle the ears of a "story-broken, busted, and disgusted generation." It requires *trust*. And that, my friend, is exactly what every believer has the ability to do. Yet, having the ability to do something and actually doing it are two different things. Why? Because our tendency is to rely on our senses, feelings, and emotions.

We are constantly tempted with the "testimony" of circumstantial evidence. In addition to the multitude of voices that are attempting to help (and although their intentions may be honorable), worldly advice can often impede God's leading in our lives. God's wisdom on how to change our story so often can be completely different from our own understanding. That's why we must trust Him. As Solomon said, "Trust the Lord with all your heart, And lean not on your own understanding; In all your ways acknowledge Him, and He shall direct your paths. Do not be wise in your own eyes. . . ." (Proverbs 3:5-7 NKJV.)

Trusting God is relying on Him, not yourself. It's simple, but it's not necessarily easy, because, we've lived most of our lives trusting flesh and blood, ourselves or others. Our biggest mistake is when we lean on our own understanding, not God's way of doing and being right. That is why our world struggles with believing, trusting, and leaning on God.

Paul the Apostle addresses this problem to the church when he says:

> *Eye has not seen, nor ear heard, Nor have entered into the heart of man The things which God has prepared for those who love Him.*
>
> *But God has revealed them to us through His Spirit. For the Spirit searches all things, yes, the deep things of God. For what man knows the things of a man except the spirit of the man which is in him? Even so no one knows the things of God except the Spirit of God. . . .*
>
> *These things we also speak, not in words which man's wisdom teaches but which the Holy Spirit*

teaches, comparing spiritual things to spiritual.
But the natural man does not receive the things of
the Spirit of God, for they are foolishness to him;
nor can he know them, because they are spiritually
discerned. But he who is spiritual judges all things,
yet he himself is rightly judged by no one. For
"who has known the mind of the Lord that he may
instruct Him?" But we have the mind of Christ.
    (1 Corinthians 2:9-16 NKJV)

What's Paul saying here? He's saying, "The Bible is a spiritual book. It's a book that requires faith in God's way of doing and being right. That's the key to changing any story—faith in God."

In Hebrews 6:12 (AMP), the definition of faith is to "[lean on God with absolute trust and confidence in Him and His power]. . . ."

To every believer, Jesus is the story changer, but He cannot change any story by violating God's undisputable law called faith. "Now faith is the substance of things hoped for, the evidence of things not seen. For by it the elders obtained a good testimony. By faith we understand that the worlds were framed by the word of God, so that the things which are seen were not made of things which are visible. . . . But without faith it is impossible to please Him, for he who comes to God must believe that He is, and that He is a rewarder of those who diligently seek Him" (Hebrews 11:1-3,6 NKJV).

Well, what do we apply our faith to in order to change our story? God's promises. Faith in God Who loves you no matter what you have been through, and Who also promises to be faithful and loyal to you with every promise given to His church. This builds hope and confidence that our best is yet to come. Paul said all of the promises of God are "yes and amen." This means that the promise of changing your story doesn't merely lie with His willingness to change your story, but also in your ability to trust, believe, and have faith in His promises.

A huge key to rewriting the story of our lives is faith. In Hebrews 6:12, it says that through faith and patience you will inherit the promises. I call these two spiritual forces *"the twins."* They need to work together. This is how an individual believer must operate to change the story of his or her city. Remember:

> *"God can change the story of a city by changing the story of one person at a time."*

When you decide to be that one person, you must also know how to operate by faith in patience so that God, by the power of the Holy Spirit, can build you up in Him. Faith and patience are real forces that must be applied—not just known about.

Sometimes when you've been damaged, hurt, broken, and are getting up from defeat and failure, the first thing God wants to do is bring healing to you: spirit, soul, and body. The instant you ask God for help, He begins to work on your behalf. Maybe you have to be restored from shaky confidence, insecurities, or some crisis. Please remember that God is loving you back to life. To change your story, begin with a solid foundation of who you are in Christ Jesus, what you have in Christ Jesus, and what the Word of God says you can do in Christ Jesus. As you develop your faith and patience in these three areas (spirit, soul, and body), you are building a rock-solid foundation.

Every person's story matters to God, including your story! We are never stuck in our stories, because Jesus is the story changer. He will rewrite the text of our lives if we open the book of our hearts.

Indeed, there are many ways to feel stuck in one's story. But through *faith and patience* in God's Word, devotions, and spending time in fellowship with like-minded people who love you, God rebuilds you from the inside out. The promises of God are helping you discover those answers. So be encouraged! God is doing a new thing in you, through you, and around you.

First, however, you must take your "Now Step." To understand what I mean by your Now Step, we must review what David said in 2 Samuel 22:

> *"God made my life complete when I placed all*
> *the pieces before him. . . . God rewrote the text of*

my life when I opened the book of my heart. . . ."
(2 Samuel 22:21 and 25 MSG)

The Now Step is reflected in this verse. Open the book of your heart. And keep it open. God won't rewrite what is not open to Him. God has amazing things to write about your life. He has plans beyond what you can ask for, hope for, or imagine on your own.

Let me remind you that when David finally opened the book of his heart, he was far from perfect. He needed forgiveness and direction. You might need the same things. God knows exactly what you need. When you yearn to get unstuck, He can show you how.

OPEN YOUR HEART AND KEEP IT OPEN. GOD WON'T REWRITE WHAT IS NOT OPEN TO HIM.

When I look at David's story, I see someone crying out for a rewrite. Think of all that had been written into his story: adultery, failure, murder, lust, and deception. These were sad facts of his history. He couldn't go back and change his past, but he refused to let his past punish his future. Instead, he took a **Now Step.** A Now Step is when you act. You do something. You move toward a destination. You don't just sit there doing nothing, wishing the story of your life would change. Remember, faith without works is dead. (See James 2:20 NKJV.) The Amplified Classic version of this verse says that faith requires corresponding actions. You don't have to live sad, mad, bitter, or angry about how things haven't gone in your favor, so far.

Here is what faith and patience do: They help you make the changes, and it begins with your Now Step.

When David opened the book of his heart—***David's Now Step***—God began to rewrite the text of his life. David didn't live in secret. He didn't try to hide anything from God. David opened the book of his heart! He became vulnerable, transparent, open, surrendered, yielding, and pliable. He didn't resist God's correction through the prophet Nathan. David's openness caused him to be humble—not hardened, defensive, or resistant. That's why David later wrote that God loves a broken and contrite heart, but that does not mean broken with sickness, disease, poverty, defeat, or anything else that the devil might do.

If you feel pessimistic about your story, I want to ask you, "Who is writing your script?" Let God. Open the book of your heart. It's not that God doesn't understand every detail of your life. It's only when you ***surrender.*** Again, opening up is about completely trusting in God. How? By trusting in what He's already promised in His Word.

Remember this Scripture: "Trust in the LORD with all your heart and lean not to your own understanding; in all your ways submit to him, and he will make your paths straight" (Proverbs 3:5-6 NIV). This is such an important concept, because God's understanding transcends our own. He thinks differently about us. He doesn't get caught up in negative thinking, as we so often do. His thoughts toward us are all about peace and love—and His desire to give us a future and a hope. Trusting God is key to your Now Step.

God wants us to enjoy amazing lives, abundant lives, lives full of love, peace, and victory. He wants to rewrite—to move your story beyond the misery and the mess-ups. God does not take pleasure in making us feel condemned, bad, guilty, inferior, or fearful. In fact, Romans 8:1-2 (NKJV) says, "There is therefore now no condemnation to those who are in Christ Jesus, who do not walk according to the flesh, but according to the Spirit. For the law of the Spirit of life in Christ Jesus has made me free from the law of sin and death." There is hope for you. There is hope for every person reading this book and following God's plan. Jesus, The Author, is still rewriting the text of our lives. our stories.

He wants to turn breakdowns into breakthroughs.

I remind you, you are Jesus' "living letter." We are living epistles (letters) known and read by all men. (See 2 Corinthians 3:2.) He loves you and is proud of you. Second Corinthians 3:3 explains that you and I are letters from Christ, not written with ink on paper, but with the Holy Spirit in our hearts. That's why God wants to change our stories for us, because we are the living testimony of God's goodness, for all to see.

That's why God loves it when someone approaches one of His children and says, "Hey, weren't you the guy in the troubled marriage?" or "Weren't you the woman in the dead-end career?"

Then comes the response: "Yes, but that was the old me. My story has changed since then! God rewrote my story because I opened the book of my heart to Him." (See Psalms 18:24.)

The bad stuff might be part of our history (and we all have history). But history does not create a compelling future. God's Word does, and He wants you to forget those things which are behind and reach forward to those things that are ahead. (See Philippians 3:13.) Again, don't let your past punish your future!

There's something very powerful about understanding faith and patience. Faith and patience working together, trusting God's promises, and persevering. These are keys to the process of rewriting your story. *"Look to yourselves (take care) that you may not (throw away or destroy) all that we and you have labored for, but that you may [persevere until you] win and receive back a perfect reward [in full]" (2 John 1:8 AMPC).*

Notice the importance of perseverance. John once said, "Persevere until you win." Hebrews encourages us to "throw off everything that hinders and the sin that so easily entangles. And let us run with perseverance the race marked out for us"

(Hebrews 12:1 NIV). Whether we know it or not, there is a race before us. Each of us must run his or her own race, not someone else's. That's what God wants. And your pace is found in God's grace. He has marked out your course, the course for an amazing life, an amazing story. Don't ever envy someone else's race. We all hear the cliché about the grass being greener on the other side of the fence. I am here to tell you: Your grass is plenty green!

To go back to our race analogy, stay in your own lane.

Speaking of lanes, I was driving with my daughter, Alexis, recently. We started talking about our visits to Singapore, Australia, and the Philippines. In Singapore and Australia, people drive on the left side of the road. In the Philippines, they drive on the right, but, before World War II, they drove on the other side. I said to her, "Alexis, in driving and in life, you have to stay in the correct lane. The way that seems right to you might not be correct." (As many American visitors to foreign countries have discovered.)

When we take care of the stuff in our own lane, we will be rewarded beyond our wildest imaginings. I reminded Alexis of a Scripture from Ephesians: "Now to Him Who, by (in consequence of) the [action of His] power that is at work within us, is able to [carry out His purpose and] do superabundantly, far over *and* above all that we [dare] ask or think [infinitely beyond our highest prayers, desires, thoughts, hopes, or dreams]—To

Him be glory in the church and in Christ Jesus throughout all generations forever and ever. Amen (so be it)" (Ephesians 3:20-21 AMPC).

I want to encourage you the way I encouraged my daughter that day. Stay in your lane. Some other lane might look faster. Yet another lane seems to be veering in a strange direction, but a lot of people are using it. Hmmm, do they know something you don't?

I know it's tempting to jump your lane. And sometimes we simply get distracted and drift out of our lanes. That can be dangerous. That's why we need to focus.

I realize that some of you reading these words right now might lack confidence, feel insecure or question whether you can go. **Yes, you can!** You wonder why God has you in *this* lane, the lane He has chosen for you. Take heart. Fulfill your destiny. Don't try to fulfill someone else's destiny. I guarantee you that there is a huge reward awaiting you at the end of your journey, the finale of your story. Jesus is there, waiting to congratulate you, saying, "Well done, good and faithful servant!"

God will not forget you. Persevere. Be patient. Remember our Scripture from Hebrews earlier in this chapter? When we are encouraged to run with patience (or perseverance), we are urged to run with *hupomone*. It is a Greek word meaning patience and endurance. It's also defined as maintaining your consistency;

being constant, day in and day out. It's a reference to being unwavering, immovable—being the same. What the force of patience does is give your developing faith time to build itself up in your spirit and time to work in you and in your circumstances.

So, a person of patience is loyal and steadfast and persevering. He or she does not swerve off-course, no matter what others are doing. Patience also helps you stay in your lane, doing the little things day in and day out. It's being faithful with what God has given you. Patience is a characteristic of the fruit of the Spirit. (See Galatians 5:22-23.)

Don't focus on all the successful people around you. Don't envy the neighborhoods they live in or the jobs they hold. Those are distractions. The enemy wants you to feel jealous and envious. Don't listen to him. Don't fall for his temptations. Resist them by faith! Peter said in 1 Peter 5:8-9 (AMPC):

> "Be well balanced (temperate, sober of mind), be vigilant and cautious at all times; for that enemy of yours, the devil, roams around like a lion roaring [in fierce hunger], seeking someone to seize upon and devour. Withstand him; be firm in faith [against his onset—rooted, established, strong, immovable, and determined], knowing that the same (identical) sufferings are appointed to your brotherhood (the whole body of Christians) throughout the world."

When the enemy starts whispering in your ear, remember Jeremiah 29: 11 (NCV). God reminds you saying, "I know what I am planning for you," says the LORD. "I have good plans for you, not plans to hurt you. I will give you hope and a good future."

Your lane holds your future and your hope. Living with patience will bring you joy. Be confident in who God made you to be. He does not make mistakes.

Look to Jesus, who is the author and finisher of our faith and our life story. Fulfill your destiny as you steadily move forward in life. Jesus is the key. It's not about your talent or good looks, even though you do look good! But our looks and abilities can fade in the future. Just ask any professional athlete who's been forced to retire. What remains, eternally, is faith in Jesus Christ.

Those of us who are parents know that we must take care when we talk to our children about their spiritual gifts. Yes, gifting is good. But people can get too enamored with their gifts. They start thinking they're "all that and a bag of chips." But open that bag, and sometimes you find nothing but air.

Again, gifting is a good thing. However, God does not need your gifts to make you great. You know what's better than gifting? Simple faithfulness. Consistency. Your gifts might get you somewhere, but your character is what *keeps* you there. And if you are not a Christ-like person of character, you could end up losing your gifts.

You could be the best speaker or teacher. You could have an amazing level of spiritual discernment. But your faith in Christ is the key to your life. Look to Jesus, not to your own gifts—and not to your neighbor's lane. If you find yourself dripping with jealousy about someone else's life, you know you need a change of heart, a change of perspective.

YOUR GIFTS CAN GET YOU TO A PLACE WHERE YOUR CHARACTER CANNOT KEEP YOU.

In fact, without faith in Jesus, it is impossible to please God. (See Hebrews 11:6.) We must have faith in the ultimate Author, the One who wants to write the wonderful stories of our lives. Let us look to the Maker of everything. The One who launched the whole universe into existence.

We have an Author who does not write with pen and ink or a computer, but by the power of the Spirit of the living God. This Author's work is permanent and glorious. The great news I want to share with you in this chapter is that God never writes off anybody! Never, ever, ever. So be patient and persevere.

And please don't be discouraged by anyone who has put you down or disowned you in some way. Yes, a person might write you off, but that person is not the author of your story. God is. And who knows what friends you might meet in the future, or what new people might join your family circle? I promise you that there are people out there who need to make contact with your goodness and love. They need the joy you can bring to their lives. And imagine the joy they can bring to your life.

I know it can hurt when someone writes us off. But that's just one person. There are more than 7 billion people on this planet. What is the opinion of one person, or even a few people? It's not about one person's opinion. The key question is, "What does God think and say?" That's what counts. Opinions are not truth. Opinions have never set a person free from bondage, trouble, tribulation, or turmoil. Jesus did. That's why He is the Way, the Truth, and the Life and why He tells us again and again that through faith and patience you shall know the truth and the truth will set you free!

You have the ultimate Author on your side. He is ready to rescript new pages of joy, new pages of God's faithfulness. God is still rewriting the text of your life, because He's promised He will never leave you nor forsake you. Yes, life can hurt sometimes, but our Creator doesn't create disaster, disease, defeat, or down days to teach you something. He, by the Holy Spirit, teaches us through His Word as we let faith and patience have their perfect work in us.

The best pages of your story are ahead of you, not behind you!

While we are on this subject, I urge you, "Don't write *yourself* off!" A divorced person might think, "I can never have a happy marriage." A person who's gone through bankruptcy might think "I can never recover financially again." A person who just went through a friendship heartbreak might think he or she can never find joy. A person who just went through a loss or crisis might say, "I just don't feel like getting up again."

There are so many ways we write ourselves off. Please don't write yourself off! Why? Because God never has. He never will! God will send people your way to breathe hope into your story. He intervenes in ways you can't imagine.

Give your story over to God. He knows how to rewrite the text of your life. He has great things to say about you.

I must say it again: God never writes off anybody. So, if He doesn't write anyone off, why would you even consider writing yourself off? Are you greater than God? Well, I know you don't think that way. That's "logic" speaking—not faith. That kind of talk is the spirit of the world, not the Spirit of God.

Remember Moses? At one point of his life, he took matters into his own hands. He wanted to do things in his timing. But his impatience and haste in the name of "rescuing" someone caused him to become a murderer. Then he ran from the authorities and became a fugitive. He ended up on the backside of the desert for 40 years—wandering, wondering, and wishing that things could be different. Maybe he thought, "I'm good for nothing. I had my chance, my opportunity, and I blew it." Maybe like you, Moses spent time pondering, "God called me, and I thought He wanted to use me. Well, maybe I was wrong. Just look at my history. Look at my past. My own people, Israel, didn't accept me. Seemingly, not even God defended me. Otherwise, why would I be here with my father-in-law Jethro on the backside of the desert?"

Or maybe Moses thought, "God wrote me off. God's mad at me. And if God wrote me off, who am I to believe in myself?"

Well, of course, those imaginations, thoughts, and inner conversations are not what God ever said or thought about Moses. And it's my conviction that while Moses was on the backside of the desert he had times of praise and worship and fellowship with God, just as David did. Perhaps one night Moses was worshipping and praising God by a campfire. Maybe it was there that God began to rewrite the text of his life as he opened the book of his heart?

We don't know for sure. But the Bible does promise this: God will always use a broken and contrite heart that is open to Him!

And what can we say about David? Mr. Adulterer. Mr. Murderer. Mr. Schemer. Ultimately, he was known as a man after God's own heart. More than 3,000 years after David's death, people still read his psalms in their Bibles. Those words are still encouraging hearts and changing lives worldwide.

David's story, like Moses's, is a powerful lesson for all of us: Don't let your mistakes stop you from believing in the great things God has planned for you. In David's case, maybe "mistake" is not a strong enough word. He made gigantic blunders. Perhaps you have too. But the Bible includes these awful things to show us that God works through open-hearted, imperfect people like us. It's a work of His grace, not our perfection or religion. He can change any story, even one that seems hopeless. Jesus came to Earth because He knew we were imperfect and could not save ourselves. We are His stories of redemption. He didn't write us off, give up on us, or throw us away in disgust. That, my friend, is God loving humanity back to life. Our stories were too bad to be fixed by anyone other than the ultimate Author, Who loved us back to life. Remember how David shared in Psalm 40:1-10 (NKJV):

> *I waited patiently for the Lord; and He inclined to me, and heard my cry.*
>
> *He also brought me up out of a horrible pit, out of the miry clay, and set my feet upon a rock, and established my steps. He has put a new song in my mouth—Praise to our God;*
>
> *Many will see it and fear, and will trust in the Lord. Blessed is that man who makes the Lord his trust, and does not respect the proud, nor such as turn aside to lies. Many, O Lord my God, are Your wonderful works which You have done; And Your thoughts toward us cannot be recounted to You*

in order; If I would declare and speak of them, They are more than can be numbered. Sacrifice and offering You did not desire; My ears You have opened.

Burnt offering and sin offering You did not require. Then I said, "Behold, I come; in the scroll of the book it is written of me. I delight to do Your will, O my God, and Your law is within my heart." I have proclaimed the good news of righteousness in the great assembly; Indeed, I do not restrain my lips, O Lord, You Yourself know. I have not hidden Your righteousness within my heart; I have declared Your faithfulness and Your salvation; I have not concealed Your lovingkindness and Your truth from the great assembly.

This is a description of David praising God for rewriting the text of his life! It's no accident that the Bible is filled with stories like David's. Remember Samson, the ladies' man? Samson was being rebellious and impulsive. He betrayed his covenant with God. It looked like he would die in shame. But when he (finally!) humbled himself and opened his heart, God made the final chapter of his life victorious. Samson had won many battles, but nothing like his epic finale.

What can I say about the Apostle Peter? He denied Jesus three times. He suffered from what I call Foot-in-Mouth Disease.

He tended to speak before he thought. He was a coward at Jesus' death, but he went on to be the courageous rock upon which the modern church was built.

Then there was Saul of Tarsus, who persecuted and antagonized the church. He imprisoned women and children. He oversaw the execution of Jesus' followers. Then God opened the book of Saul's heart. He rewrote his story so vigorously that even Saul's name changed—to Paul, the apostle.

These stories still happen today, and through faith and patience in Jesus Christ you are a qualified candidate. I recently met a young man who had received the Lord, but was going through difficult times. His family life was suffering, and he decided he wanted a divorce. He knew it would devastate his wife and their three beautiful children, but it seemed there was no other way out. He was on the way to the courthouse, divorce documents in hand.

He reached the courthouse steps. Then, as he would describe it later, "Something stopped me. I just couldn't go through with it." He called his wife, who told him she had been praying for him. Within hours, they were meeting with pastors at our church for counseling.

And today? All I can say is that God is awesome. He is bringing this family a breakthrough through His healing and restoration.

This reminds me of another recent story. I was speaking in Santa Barbara, CA. I concluded with an altar call, and a man approached me. "Do you know who I am?" he asked me.

"You do look really familiar," I said, as I studied his face.

"That's because I'm your cousin!"

My mother's brother, my uncle, was this man's father. Growing up, we had lived . . . let me just call it a scattered and very difficult life.

This man's brother, whom I used to run around with, was found dead in a river bed, after an overdose.

But even after all that went on in my cousin's life, God never wrote him off.

Please don't write yourself off. And don't write off others. James says, "My dear friends, if you know people who have wandered off from God's truth, don't write them off. Go after them. Get them back and you will have rescued precious lives from destruction. . . ." (James 5:19-20 MSG).

Listen to the Holy Spirit speak to you about yourself and others. We all know people who want to write themselves off. They want to give up. Throw in the towel. And maybe it's because they wandered off. You know, there's more than one way to "wander off." Maybe you know someone who wandered off by just being disappointed with life, as life's pressure got to be too overwhelming. Maybe there's a person who wandered off by temptation or sin or bad associations. Or, maybe they got into erroneous doctrine. Maybe some wandered off because of a loss in the family, or feeling of rejection, or loss of hope. The list can go on and on and on.

James clearly states that "wandering off" isn't God's will. No one will ever find true fulfillment or happiness by wandering off. Why? Because James says they wandered "from the truth." Not only from Jesus, Who is *"The Truth"* and the only begotten Son of God. They have also wandered from the truth of trusting in God's promises. Why do I know this? Because God's Word is truth, the truth that can set them free. (See John 8:31-32.) God takes no pleasure in seeing people walk in sadness—broke, busted, disgusted, sick, diseased, oppressed, dejected, hopeless, helpless, and broken-hearted. We know this because he tells the church: *Don't write them off!*

In other words, don't give up on them. He instructs us to go after them—get them back! Here's why: Get ready for this. It's because of how He sees us. That's why we can't give up on people or ourselves. Remember what James said, "[A]nd you will have rescued precious lives from destruction." Did you hear that? God calls you precious. You are of great value to him. You are not to be treated carelessly. This is how God sees you, even if you did wander off from the truth, and consider yourself imperfect and unworthy. His view of you, others, and their stories is that we are "precious lives." Wow! That's what gives us reason to live, hope, be passionate, excited, and joyful.

So, we can help change others' stories, as well as our own. I love the simple command in the verse above: "Get them back." Recapture them with God's love. Rescue them with *compassion*. Rescue is not based on one's talents, good works, good looks, lovability, gift, ability, or anything else. Are there people in your life whom you've written off—an auntie, uncle, brother, sister, boss, or friend? Or ex-friend? If so, open your heart.

Our hearts should be in synch with God's. He does not write people off. He sees the glimmer of hope in the darkest story. He saw hope in us, even when our stories seemed hopeless. The enemy loves it when someone gives up all hope. But God can step in by sending others to us, to speak to our hearts. And I want you to understand, if you'll

THE BEST PAGES OF YOUR STORY ARE YET TO BE WRITTEN.

just keep the book of your heart open, no matter where you've been or what you've done, God will be there for you. The best pages of your story are yet to be written. Perhaps, and I don't doubt it at all, some of you who are holding this book right now.

God is looking for only one thing: an open heart. He's never written off your dream. He's never put you on the back burner. Keep the book of your heart open. He has a message for you:

"I am still writing on your behalf." Remember, through faith and patience you will inherit the promise. Take your Now Step. Trust God and His Word, for you are a precious life in the story of God.

A Fresh Start

I came from abject poverty. I came from a life that had nothing. I was a child of a broken family. As a young boy, I stood at the living room door—the one with the screen falling off—and watched my father walk away from our family. He left our home in California to return to Mexico. He left my mother, my sister, and me behind.

As I watched my father walk away, I kept hoping he would turn around and at least wave good-bye. He never looked back, even though he knew we were standing there, waiting.

So I know what it's like to experience abandonment and rejection. I understand poverty. I know what it's like to struggle through life. I know what it's like to battle doubt, to endure broken dream after broken dream. My broken dream came out of a broken home—a dysfunctional home with a lot of pain and hurt. But because my experience was ingrained in everyday life, it was what I considered normal.

But today I know what it's like to paint a new picture on the canvas of my heart—then see elements in that picture take on shape and color. I know how it feels to have my story changed by Jesus, the Story Changer.

My story began with . . .

A father who never gave love. My mother had to raise her son and daughter single-handedly, basically. My father went off on a "world tour." I don't say that to discredit him. I say it to define and clarify my situation for you. My father was heartless toward my mother and unloving toward his children. He never shared any love or compassion with us. He never cared for anyone but himself. Until he got saved (thank You, Jesus!), he was the most selfish individual walking the planet Earth.

So my mother was a sole provider who did the job of two parents. She came over from Mexico and raised me and my sister in a very difficult and hostile environment. When she came to the United States, she did not know English and did not have a job skill, per se. So she worked the fields, picking lettuce, lemons, tomatoes, and things like that. Eventually, she was able to put herself through night school and learn some English. She then began to develop skills in electronics. She learned a particular skill set to get our family to a better level of economics. I am sure that a lot of moms reading this book made similar choices and sacrifices. Your kids have seen you make those sacrifices. Maybe they didn't understand it at the time, but God will bring it to their remembrance. They will remember the sacrifices, the concessions, and the tough decisions you had to make to bring your children a better life.

A dream of something better, someday.

When I was young, I got frustrated that one could dream, but then fail to see things change in my home and in my life. But I didn't understand that change doesn't happen without effort.

Eventually, I came to better understand the power of a dream. A dream starts like a little apple seed. It looks so small and insignificant. But it can grow and grow. One single seed grows into a beautiful tree bursting with fruit. One tree becomes two. Before long, you have an entire orchard that can feed thousands. This is why we need to embrace our dreams and work toward them. This is why we need to have hope in our stories.

Because of what I have learned in my life, I promise you that your faith in God can transform your story. It will turn your world around. Faith is the only force that will lift you out of your circumstances and transcend your own abilities. Faith will move your story past all the failures, past all the doubting voices you might hear.

As I lived out my story, I cannot even count how many people continued to doubt me and denigrate the dream God gave me. It's not just that people refused to help me; they actually worked against me. They wouldn't join me when I needed a partner. They said all kinds of negative things to me, and about me. Sometimes, I did not get an opportunity because I was "the brown guy," the "Mexican guy." So I was looked at a certain way. Even well-intentioned family members added to the negativity—with some wrong-headed teachings.

FAITH DOES NOT STAY KNOCKED DOWN. FAITH GETS UP AND CONTINUES ON THE PATH. FAITH KEEPS WRITING YOUR UNIQUE STORY.

But God was my helper and my guide. He was the one rewriting the text of my life, as I opened my heart to Him. He was transforming me by renewing my mind. All of the negativity only served to stir up my faith. Faith does not stay knocked down. Faith gets up and continues on the path. Faith keeps writing your unique story.

In high school, I worked hard as a student and an athlete. I graduated from high school, then from the University of Southern California with a degree in architecture. I was fortunate to receive a soccer scholarship to help pay for my college education.

At USC, I had a perfectly good dream: I wanted to be the most successful Latino architect in the world. However, during my junior year, I started my relationship with God, through faith in Jesus Christ.

After graduating, I worked for several years as an architect in California and Hawaii. My faith actually intensified my drive to be tops in my field. I thought this would honor the One Who gave me my abilities and desires. However, as years passed, I began to notice different desires emerging on the canvas of my heart. God was working something inside of me. I felt a tug toward a new and different chapter of my story.

At first, I was perturbed to feel my passion for architecture waning. But I had made a choice to avoid compartmentalizing my spiritual life. God was not relegated to Sunday mornings only. "God," I prayed, "if You are real, then You are real in all areas of my life. Show me what You want me to do."

My faith was strong, but I did not want to be involved in "the ministry." I had no desire to be a missionary in some far-off land (which was my definition of "the ministry" back then). More important, I doubted my abilities. I knew my limitations.

"What can I possibly do in ministry?" I wondered. "What do I have to offer? I don't know what to say to people about God and faith."

So I started to wonder if I was truly hearing something from God. That's where many people stop in their stories. They listen to their doubts. Then they talk themselves out of the desires of their hearts.

I am not saying that if you devote your life to God, all your goals are going to change. You will abandon your career and go into some form of ministry. No, my point is this: Be open to a Dream Shift, a new chapter in your story as you trust the One who knows what is best for your life.

Meanwhile, my passion for architecture continued to drain out of me. Conversely, my love for other people and my desire to serve them began to grow. God was changing me from the inside out.

I kept moving forward in my story, working the new dream God had given me. The Bible says, in Ecclesiastes 5:3 NKJV, "For a dream comes through much activity."

I was on a journey. I knew where I wanted to go. I had an image of my destination. But I didn't just wander around in the wind. I took one purposeful step at a time. Dreams unfold day by day. Our stories are written one page at a time. What you do today prepares you for tomorrow.

Remember, too, that God wants you to succeed even more than you want it. Too many people pray, "Please, please, God. Just let me fulfill my dream!" They pray as if God is their opponent. God is not your obstacle. Your dream is a gift from Him. Your dream is never about just you. That's why many people fail. They think it's all about them.

Yes, your dreams involve you and bless you. But if a dream is truly from God, it will touch other lives in positive ways. The

Giver of Dreams, the Ultimate Author, wants you to flourish and prosper. He wants others to flourish and prosper as well. As we've discovered in this book, our stories are connected. Our dreams are connected with other dreamers. We need to connect with these people for mutual inspiration and help. We all need what each other brings to the table. We need to disciple, and to be discipled.

Psalms 92:13 (NKJV) says:

> *"Those who are planted in the house of the Lord*
> *Shall flourish in the courts of our God."*

The giver of dreams wants you to flourish. He wants you to prosper. There is no question about that.

As you make your journey, understand that your dreams are connected with other dreamers who are walking by faith. You need to be connected to these people.

Your dream, your story, is a gift from God. He will provide all that you need to succeed. The power is there, if only you will seek it. Invite the Lord into your story. We must look to Him, not our own abilities, to complete our stories. A story succeeds when it is built by faith. Faith changes stories. Faith makes dreams come true.

God alone has the power and wisdom to change your story from bad to great, or even from great to amazing. He is the key.

Sometimes we think we know better. Well, we don't. I learned this as my career path changed. God is the Creator; we are the created. We sometimes cannot see beyond our own circumstances. God can.

I left the architecture profession. God helped me and my wife, Kuna, found a small church of 25 people. Today, more than 30 years later, God has blessed Word of Life Christian Center. We are now able to serve people in the Hawaiian Islands, as well as in California and Japan. This growth is not about my talents. It's about what God can do with our stories if we follow Him.

I urge you to discover how God can rewrite your story.

The love of God be with you. Thank you for letting me share in your story. Because you have read this book, you and I are partners in our stories. For this I am grateful. Our best is yet to come.

word of life Christian Center was founded by Pastors Art and Kuna Sepúlveda on Sunday, September 23rd, 1984, at Central Middle School in Honolulu, with twenty-five (25) people in attendance. Since the very beginning, Pastors Art and Kuna have held forth a message of victorious living through faith in God—the "word of life" (Philippians 2:16).

Over the past 3 decades, Word of Life has grown and expanded from a single church in downtown Honolulu to many locations across the state and the Pacific.

It is our commitment to reach out to "win souls and make disciples" locally and globally. In the state of Hawaii, we have hundreds of Life Groups (small group Bible studies) to help people connect to God and to our church family.

Word of Life also has church plants in California (Santa Barbara and San Francisco, with more on the way). One of the newest church plants is located in Yokohama, Japan.

Word of Life's vision continues to encourage and inspire us to reach people and touch lives! Our goal is to reach the 44 nations of the Pacific Rim and beyond!

For more information about Pastor Art Sepúlveda and Word of Life Christian Center, please visit us online at: wordoflifehawaii.com.